CW00684526

I WANT to
MAKE my
HOME IN YOU

"Come, follow me"
Catechetical resources
Notre Dame de Vie Institute

I Want to Make My Home in You

Preparation for the sacraments
of reconciliation and the Eucharist

Children's book
Maguy Bagnol, Marie-Thérèse Rineau and Benoît Caulle

Illustrations
Suzy Dumont

Published by Redemptorist Publications
Wolf's Lane, Chawton, Hampshire, GU34 3HQ, UK
Tel. +44 (0)1420 88222, Fax. +44 (0)1420 88805
Email rp@rpbooks.co.uk, www.rpbooks.co.uk

A registered charity limited by guarantee
Registered in England 03261721

Copyright © Redemptorist Publications 2018
Second printing 2019

First published November 2016
by © Éditions du Carmel – Toulouse – France
Je Veux Demeurer Chez Toi: ISBN 978-2-84713-431-5

Text by Maguy Bagnol, Marie-Thérèse Rineau and Benoît Caulle
© Translated from French to English by Sr Hyacinthe Defos du Rau OP

Edited by Rachel Thompson and Sr Hyacinthe Defos du Rau OP
English edition – designed by Eliana Thompson
and artwork by Peena Lad

Illustrated by Suzy Dumont
© Association Talitha Koum – 84210 – Venasque, France

ISBN 978-0-85231-490-6

A CIP catalogue record for this book is available from
the British Library.

Nihil Obstat: Rev. Dr Brendan Killeen BSc., STB, MA, JCL, MCL, PhD
Censor Deputatus

Imprimatur: + Peter Doyle
Bishop of Northampton
Northampton December 2017

The Nihil Obstat and Imprimatur are a declaration that a book or pamphlet is
considered to be free from doctrinal or moral error. It is not implied that those who
have granted the Nihil Obstat and Imprimatur agree with the contents.

Printed by Orchard Press, Cheltenham Ltd.

Contents

To you,
who are preparing to receive Jesus,

you have just been given this book: *I want to make my home in you.*
Listen attentively to these words that Jesus is saying to you:
"I want to make my home in you."
Jesus is calling you and inviting you to a closer friendship with him.
What about you?
Do you really want Jesus to "make his home in you"?
Do you want to follow him more closely?

With your catechesis group and the help of the adults around you,
you will prepare yourself to meet Jesus in the sacraments of reconciliation and the Eucharist.

Since the beautiful day of your baptism, God has been living in you.
The sacraments are the most precious gifts that Jesus offers us.
Through them, Jesus continues the work he began when he was among his people:
he heals, forgives, feeds and comforts all those who come to him.

Through the sacrament of reconciliation, you will receive Jesus' forgiveness.
Light, peace and joy will fill your heart.

Through the sacrament of the Eucharist, Jesus, the Bread of Life, will give himself to you
to help you grow as a child of God

As you open this book, open your heart to Jesus: he is the one speaking to you.

After each meeting, you will find in this book a summary of what you have experienced during each session with the group:

- the title: this is a word of the Gospel for you today
- the "word of God": you can read it again to grow in your friendship with Jesus
- "I welcome the word of God": this explanation of the word will help you to deepen your understanding of it and receive it with faith and love
- "The Word of God in my life": you will find suggestions for activities, and sometimes games to play
- "I commit myself": you make a decision and you commit yourself to live it;
- "I remember": you retain a word of the Gospel as Mary did, keeping all these things in her heart;
- On a colourful page, you will find: "I pray" and "I sing"; the text of the prayer can help you to be faithful to your meetings with the Lord each day.

Jesus himself will gradually reveal to you how he wants to live in your heart. Listen to him! Your desire to receive him will grow as you listen to his word. What great joy it is for him to fill you with his love!

Do not be afraid to open wide the doors of your heart to Jesus!

The journey towards the sacrament of reconciliation

I prepare my heart
to welcome the mercy
and forgiveness
of Jesus

THIS IS MY SON, THE BELOVED

1. BAPTISM

Baptism:
the beginning of my Christian life.

THE WORD OF GOD

MATTHEW 3:1-2. 5-6. 13-17

[01] In due course, John the Baptist appeared. He preached in the wilderness of Judaea and this was his message: [02] "Repent for the kingdom of heaven is close at hand!" [05] Then Jerusalem and all Judea and the whole Jordan district made their way to him, [06] and, as they were baptised by him in the river Jordan they confessed their sins...

[...] [13] Then Jesus appeared: he came from Galilee to the Jordan to be baptised by John. [14] John tried to dissuade him, "it is I who need baptism from you" he said, "and yet you come to me!" [15] But Jesus replied, "Leave it like this for the time being; it is fitting that we should, in this way, do all that righteousness demands". At this, John gave in to him.

[16] As soon as Jesus was baptised, he came up from the water, and suddenly the heavens opened and he saw the Spirit of God descending like a dove, and coming down on him. [17] And a voice spoke from heaven, "This is my Son, the Beloved; my favour rests on him."

MATTHEW 28: 19

[19] "Go, therefore, make disciples of all the nations; baptise them in the name of the Father and of the Son and of the Holy Spirit"

MARK16:16

[16] "[The one] who believes and is baptised will be saved"

I welcome the word of God

On the banks of the river Jordan, John the Baptist, the prophet, is calling everyone to a baptism of conversion. He announces, and is preparing for, the coming of the Messiah. Jesus slips in among the crowd so that he too may receive baptism. Jesus chooses to be with sinners so that he can share our human condition and save us.

By coming on earth, Jesus "opened the heavens". He has made it possible for people to open themselves up again to the never ending love of God: Jesus is the Saviour, "the Lamb of God who takes away the sins of the world".

The Spirit comes down on Jesus to complete with him the wonderful work of a new creation: the creation of the children of God.

REPENT

THE HEAVENS OPENED

HE SAW THE SPIRIT OF GOD COMING DOWN ON HIM

THIS IS MY SON, THE BELOVED; MY FAVOUR RESTS ON HIM

Until now, Jesus was only known as the son of Mary, and the son of Joseph the carpenter. But even before he became the son of Mary, Jesus was the eternal Son of the Father. The Son has been with the Father from all eternity. Jesus is God, God from God.

Today, on the banks of the river Jordan, God shows himself to us. He reveals himself as:

- **Father:** a Father filled with love for his Son
- **Son:** the Beloved, the joy of the Father
- **Holy Spirit:** love of the Father and the Son
- One God, three persons.

This is the mystery of the Trinity!

The word of God in my life

Write down what was said about Jesus at his baptism.

....

....

....

Write down what happens when Jesus comes up out of the water.

....

....

What is the most precious gift of your baptism?

....

....

I DECIDE how I will respond to the commitment of my baptism:

....

....

I REMEMBER:

Through baptism, we become children of the Father,
in the image of Jesus, his beloved Son,
under the guidance of the Holy Spirit.
We belong to the Church,
the family of all who are baptised.

My baptism

I was baptised on the: ..../...................../.....................

in the parish of : ....

I can put a picture of my baptism here

On that day, the priest said to me:

" ...., I baptise you in

the name of the FATHER, and of the SON

and of the HOLY SPIRIT."

I pray

My God, you give me your life.
I am so happy to be your child!
Like Jesus, I can call you "Father".
You love me and I belong to you!

Jesus, you are the beloved Son of
    the Father,
you are the Lamb of God, the Saviour.
I want to look at you and listen to you.
Make me a true child of God.

Holy Spirit, Spirit of Love,
    you have been living in me since my baptism.
Help me to be aware of your presence,
and teach me how to follow Jesus.

Glory to you, God,
Father, Son and Holy Spirit!

I sing

Father, I adore you

COME, FOLLOW ME

2. THE CALL TO BECOME A DISCIPLE

Jesus calls us to become his friends

THE WORD OF GOD

MATTHEW 4:18-22

[18] As [Jesus] was walking by the Sea of Galilee, he saw two brothers, Simon, who was called Peter, and his brother Andrew; they were making a cast in the lake with their net, for they were fishermen. [19] And he said to them, "Follow me and I will make you fishers of men." [20] And they left their nets at once and followed him. [21] Going on from there, he saw another pair of brothers, James son of Zebedee, and his brother John; they were in their boat with their father Zebedee, mending their nets, and he called them. [22] At once, leaving the boat and their father, they followed him.

MATTHEW 19: 16-17. 19-22

[16] There was a man who came to him and asked, "Master, what good deed must I do to possess eternal life?" [17] Jesus said to him, "Why do you ask me about what is good? There is one alone who is good. But if you wish to enter into life, keep the commandments." [...] [19] Honour your father and mother [...] love your neighbour as yourself." [20] The young man said to him, "I have kept all these. What more do I need to do?" [21] Jesus said, "If you wish to be perfect, go and sell what you own, and give the money to the poor, and you will have treasure in heaven; then come, follow me." [22] But when the young man heard these words he went away sad, for he was a man of great wealth.

I welcome the word of God

Jesus calls Peter and Andrew, James and John, and invites them to follow him. They are the first four disciples of the group of twelve. Jesus chooses them to be "fishers of men", so that in their turn they may call other people who will love Jesus and follow him. What an amazing mission Jesus has entrusted to them!

The Gospel says "At once" they left everything! What a quick response! They do not stop to discuss it. They do not make Jesus wait for them. They follow Jesus immediately.

These disciples are so generous! They do not count the cost. They love Jesus more than anything. These fishermen want to live with Jesus, listen to his words and learn to love like him. So they become disciples of Jesus.

COME, FOLLOW ME

THEY LEFT THEIR NETS AT ONCE AND FOLLOWED HIM

The young man asks an important question. He is anxious to do what is right. Jesus reminds him that God alone is good and the source of everything that is good. Jesus invites him not to be satisfied with simply obeying the commandments but to love God and other people with all his heart. Jesus calls the young man to holiness, to a greater and deeper love. Jesus calls him to leave everything, like John, Andrew and the twelve, and to follow him.

Jesus does not force the young man, he respects his freedom: "if you wish". Jesus gives him the key to entering into eternal life: it is to give everything. It is now up to him to open his heart, but faced with the challenge of what Jesus is asking – "sell what you own, and give the money to the poor; and you will have treasure in heaven. Then come, follow me" – the young man goes away sad. Yet Jesus could have made him truly happy because Jesus himself is the treasure which is more precious than all the young man's wealth.

WHAT GOOD DEED MUST I DO TO POSSESS ETERNAL LIFE?

IF YOU WISH, YOU WILL HAVE TREASURE

COME, FOLLOW ME

The word of God in my life

Jesus calls me by name

"You also, _____ , come, follow me"

(Write your name)

This word of Jesus to his disciples: "Come, follow me" is for me today. Along with all those who are baptised and belong to the family of the Church, I am also called to follow Jesus, to believe in him, to choose him freely and to love him.

What is the word hidden in the middle blocks?

....

1. Simon's brother
2. scaly sea creature
3. used to catch fish
4. invited
5. where Jesus lived
6. Simon's other name
7. to walk behind someone
8. large area of fresh water
9. large expanse of salt water

Make up a sentence using as many words as possible from the grid

....

....

....

....

Jesus calls us in many ways. List a few examples.

....

....

....

I COMMIT MYSELF:

This is the place where I can put the footprint on which I have written how I will follow Jesus and how I will respond to his love.

I REMEMBER:

I choose a passage from the Gospel and write it down, to help me keep it in my heart:

....

....

....

I pray

Jesus,
you called James and John,
Andrew, Peter, and many others...
You said to them: "Come, follow me".

You are also calling me by name.
You know me and you love me.
You look at me and you say to me:
"Come, follow me".

Jesus,
you are waiting for my answer.
Help me to be as generous
as your first disciples.

Yes, Jesus, I want to follow you,
I want to be your friend.
Jesus, you are my greatest treasure.
With you, I have everything.

I sing

Follow Me, follow Me

OUR FATHER WHO ART IN HEAVEN

3. WE PRAY WITH JESUS

I look at Jesus who is praying and I pray with him

THE WORD OF GOD

MATTHEW 6:9-13

[09] So you should pray like this:
Our Father in heaven,
may your name be held holy,
[10] your kingdom come,
your will be done, on earth as in heaven.
[11] Give us today, our daily bread.
[12] And forgive us our debts,
as we have forgiven those who are in debt to us.
[13] And do not put us to the test,
but save us from the evil one.

MATTHEW 6:6

[06] "When you pray, go to your private room and, when you have shut your door,
pray to your Father who is in that secret place;
and your Father who sees all that is done in secret will reward you."

I welcome the word of God

Jesus, Son of God, learnt to pray in the midst of his human family. Like every Jewish child, he prayed the ancient prayer of his people: "Shema Israel", "Hear, O Israel, the Lord our God is one God". Jesus would go to the synagogue in Nazareth every Sabbath, to praise God and to listen to his word.

During his public life, Jesus prayed a lot. The disciples saw their master spending long hours in prayer. Sometimes he would spend the night in prayer, or he would go out very early in the morning to a deserted place to pray. One of Jesus' disciples asked him:"

"Lord, teach us to pray."

Jesus answered them: "When you pray, say: Our Father in heaven"

Jesus, the only Son, turns to his Father in love and finds his joy in him. This is the secret of Jesus' prayer. This will be the secret of the disciples' prayer: to welcome the Father's love like a child filled with complete trust, which snuggles up in his or her father's arms saying: "Abba! Daddy!"

In the first three petitions of the Our Father, Jesus calls his disciples to focus their attention on the glory of the Father: the holiness of his name, the coming of his kingdom and the fulfilment of his will.

In the last four petitions, Jesus hands all our human needs and worries to the neverending love of his Father. God is the "Father of mercies" from whom all good things come. In total trust, the disciples can expect everything they need from this Father full of goodness.

LORD, TEACH US TO PRAY

OUR FATHER, WHO ART IN HEAVEN

The word of God in my life

I choose one of the petitions of the Our Father. What does it mean for me?

....

....

....

....

....

To enter into prayer...

1. I leave behind ....

2. I find a quiet ....

3. I make the ....

4. I call on the ....

5. I read a passage from the ....

6. I close ....

- my eyes
- sign of the cross
- Gospel
- my activities
- Holy Spirit
- and silent place

My moments of prayer during the day

in the church   ✳   I offer my day to God

in the morning   ✳   I give thanks to God and ask him to forgive me

in the evening   ✳   I remember to turn to God

in the midst of my activities   ✳   I find Jesus present in the tabernacle

I choose ✓ and I COMMIT MYSELF

- ❑ to praying the Our Father every evening
- ❑ to setting apart a moment for silent prayer in a quiet place
- ❑ to praying as a family or with my brothers and sisters
- ❑ to being more attentive during Sunday Mass.

I learn by heart the prayer of the Our Father.

I REMEMBER:

I choose a passage from the Gospel and I write it down, to help me keep it in my heart:

"Go to your room...
pray to your Father who is in that secret place; and your
Father will reward you."

I sing

Abba Father,

Father

In silence and peace, come and meet the living God

I pray

Our Father, who art in heaven
hallowed be thy name;
thy kingdom come,
thy will be done,
on earth as it is in heaven.
Give us this day our daily bread,
and forgive us our trespasses,
as we forgive those who trespass against us;
and lead us not into temptation,
but deliver us from evil.
Amen.

With Jesus
I am happy to be able to call you "Father",
and to know that I am your child.
May your kingdom come in my heart
and in every heart.
May I always do your will, like Jesus.
May your love fill my life
and may it teach me to forgive.
Deliver me from everything that is bad.
May your grace in me
be stronger than sin!
May your Holy Spirit transform me
and lead me to you! Amen.

LOVE THE LORD YOUR GOD AND YOUR NEIGHBOUR AS YOURSELF

4. WE LOVE LIKE JESUS

I look at how Jesus loves and I love like him

THE WORD OF GOD

LUKE 10: 25-37

[25] There was a lawyer who, to disconcert Jesus, stood up and said to him, "Master, what must I do to inherit eternal life?" [26] He said to him, "What is written in the Law? What do you read there?" [27] He replied, "You must love the Lord your God with all your heart, with all your soul, with all your strength and with all your mind, and your neighbour as yourself." [28] "You have answered right," said Jesus, "do this and life is yours."

[29] But the man was anxious to justify himself and said to Jesus, "And who is my neighbour?" [30] Jesus replied, "A man was once on his way down from Jerusalem to Jericho, and fell into the hands of brigands; they took all he had, beat him and Then made off, leaving him half-dead. [31] Now a priest happened to be travelling Down the same road, but when he saw the man, he passed by on the other side. [32] In the same way a Levite who came to the place saw him, and passed by on the other side. [33] But a Samaritan traveller who came upon him was moved with compassion when he saw him. [34] He went up, and bandaged his wounds; pouring oil and wine on them. He then lifted him on to his own mount, carried him to the inn and looked after him. [35] Next day, he took out two denarii and handed them to the innkeeper. "Look after him," he said "and on my way back I will make good any extra expense you have."

[36] "Which of these three, do you think, proved himself neighbour to the man who fell into the brigands' hands?" [37] "The one who took pity on him," he replied. Jesus said to him, "Go and do the same yourself."

I welcome the word of God

By becoming one of us, Jesus revealed the Father's infinite love. He showed God's love for everyone through his words and actions. Now Jesus explains to us, by using a parable, how we should love each other.

The teacher of the Law has a good knowledge of all the commandments given by God to Moses: "You must love God with all your heart...You must love your neighbour as yourself." Yet he wants to know more:

THE PARABLE OF THE GOOD SAMARITAN

"Master, who is my neighbour?" Jesus welcomes his question. He invites the lawyer to think about it by telling him the story of a man who fell into the hands of robbers.

He saw him and passed by. Jesus first points out that the priest and the Levite avoided the man who was suffering. They showed him no act of kindness.

YOU MUST LOVE YOUR NEIGHBOUR AS YOURSELF

The Samaritan however, was a foreigner, a traveller. Yet he saw him and was moved with compassion. The Samaritan looked at him and let himself be affected by the suffering of this man who was alone and wounded.

He went over to him. He became his neighbour. Filled with pity, the Samaritan gave him all his time, he spent money on the man's healing without worrying about the cost, he took complete care of him.

The good Samaritan is Jesus himself. He was with the Father in his glory. He saw the misery of his people wounded by sin. So that he might come close to them, God became man. He feeds his people with his word to satisfy their hunger. He lays his hands on the people who are the sick to heal them. He comforts those who sorrowful and blesses the children. Jesus loves each person with God's own love.

The word of God in my life

I am "the neighbour" of lots of people. Here are their names:

....

....

....

I can write down here the names of saints who have done works of charity:

The most important thing is charity. Only love will matter when we get to heaven and are with God. God will not look at whether we have done extraordinary things. God wants us to do everything, even the smallest things, out of love.

I COMMIT MYSELF to being a good Samaritan.

I can highlight in this list what I am going to do this week:

- I will show respect for other people by what I do and say.
- I will serve others and make them happy.
- I will share with others and lend things to them; I will give cheerfully.
- I will be welcoming and comfort others, and not leave anyone out.
- I will forgive.
- I will not try to get my own back or retaliate.

I KEEP IN MIND this word of God.

I colour it.

you must love God
with all your heart...
and your neighbour
as yourself.

I pray

Jesus, you are the true "good Samaritan",
you have pity on those who are sick, on sinners,
    and on all those who search for you.
You come close to each one of us.
You love us so much
that you give your life for us.

O Jesus,
I want to love like you.
Give me your Spirit of love.
Strengthen me.
Help me, like you, to know how to come close
    to those who are suffering,
to those who are waiting for a look
or an act of kindness.
Teach me how to welcome
those who are different from me,
those who upset me.

Jesus, help me to recognise your presence in
    everyone and love them all, as you do.

I sing

Love the Lord your God

I HAVE COME FROM HEAVEN TO DO THE WILL OF MY FATHER

5. WE OBEY LIKE JESUS

I look at the obedience of Jesus and I obey like him

THE WORD OF GOD

JOHN 6:38

[38] "I have come from heaven, not to do my own will, but to do the will of the one who sent me."

MATTHEW 12:46-50

[46] [Jesus] was still speaking to the crowds when his mother and his brothers appeared; they were standing outside and were anxious to have a word with him. [47] But to the man who told him this [48] Jesus replied, "Who is my mother? Who are my brothers?" [49] And stretching out his hand towards his disciples he said, "Here are my mother and my brothers. [50] Anyone who does the will of my Father in heaven is my brother and sister and mother."

I welcome the word of God

With a "yes" full of love for his Father, Jesus accepts his mission as Saviour. He comes down from heaven to earth and becomes a little child so that he could be close to us. In Nazareth, Jesus does the will of his Father by obeying Mary and Joseph. He obeys the laws of the Jewish people to whom he belongs and he goes to pray in the synagogue.

During the three years of his preaching, Jesus is guided by the Holy Spirit.

He always seeks to do what pleases his Father, as he says in his prayer: "Not my will, but your will be done." Jesus' loving obedience takes him all the way to the cross. There he saves all people from their refusal to love and restores them to friendship with God.

ANYONE WHO DOES THE WILL OF MY FATHER IS MY BROTHER AND SISTER AND MOTHER

Jesus, the perfect model of obedience, teaches the crowds how important it is to obey God. He points to his disciples who are gathered near him and he looks at them; he knows them well: they are his friends, the ones he has chosen. They have responded to his call. The disciples listen to Jesus' word and learn from him how to obey the Father. By obeying, they are more like Jesus and become his brothers. They are children of the heavenly Father. What a joy it is for them to belong to the family of Jesus!

I HAVE COME FROM HEAVEN TO DO THE WILL OF THE ONE WHO SENT ME

In this new family that Jesus has gathered round him, Mary has a special place. She draws the disciples into her own obedience. Mary is the one who has always said "yes" to God, the one who keeps the words of Jesus in her heart and lives by them. Mary is both the mother and a disciple of Jesus.

The word of God in my life

I can answer the questions here (you will find help by looking again at the texts):

Why did Jesus come down on earth? ....

Who does Jesus let himself be led by? ....

What is the attitude that will help me to be like Jesus? ....

What does Mary say to the servants at the wedding?..

Whom should we obey? ....

....

From these examples, underline what you think is the best kind of obedience

＊　　Lucy obeys because she is afraid of being told off.

＊　　Tom only obeys when he is promised a reward.

＊　　Gabriel obeys so that he can make Jesus happy.

＊　　Hannah only answers after her mum has asked her three times.

＊　　Sebastian says "yes" but in the end does exactly what he wants.

＊　　Jessica first argues but then, in the end, obeys.

Explain your choice:

....

....

....

I COMMIT MYSELF this week to showing my love for Jesus by being more willing to obey when:

....

....

I REMEMBER:

Anyone who does the will of my Father
is my brother and sister and mother

I sing

Trust and obey

I pray

Jesus, you always do what pleases your Father.
You show him your love
by obeying Mary and Joseph
and yet you are God!
From Bethlehem to the Cross,
you do as your Father asks.
Through your obedience, you have saved us!
Jesus, I ask you to forgive me
for all the times I have disobeyed.

Father, how I want to be like Jesus!
Bend my heart to do your will:
so that I can truly be your child
and bring you joy.

Holy Spirit, lead me!
Be my light and my strength
so that I may always do as the Father asks,
like Jesus.

MY CHILD, YOUR SINS ARE FORGIVEN

6. THE PARALYSED MAN

I welcome the forgiveness of Jesus

THE WORD OF GOD

MARK 2:1-12

[01] When [Jesus] returned to Capernaum some time later, word went round that he was back; [02] and so many people collected that there was no room left, even in front of the door. He was preaching the word to them [03] when some people came bringing him a paralytic carried by four men, [04] but as the crowd made it impossible to get the man to him, they stripped the roof over the place where Jesus was; and when they had made an opening, they lowered the stretcher on which the paralytic lay. [05] Seeing their faith, Jesus said to the paralytic, "My child, your sins are forgiven."

[06] Now, some scribes were sitting there, and they thought to themselves, [07] "How can this man talk like that? He is blaspheming. Who can forgive sins but God?" [08] Jesus, inwardly aware that this was what they were thinking, said to them, "Why do you have these thoughts in your hearts? [09] Which of these is easier: to say to the paralytic, 'Your sins are forgiven,' or to say, 'Get up, pick up your stretcher and walk?' [10] But to prove to you that the Son of Man has authority on earth to forgive sins." - [11] he said to the paralytic - [11] "I order you: get up, pick up your stretcher and go off home."

[12] And the man got up, picked up his stretcher at once and walked out in front of everyone, so that they were all astounded and praised God, saying, "We have never seen anything like this!"

I welcome the word of God

The people have heard about Jesus. News about the miracles he has performed has been passed around. The people look to Jesus in the hope that he will give them a life-giving word and healing.

Jesus, who knows what they are thinking and how much they want to be healed too, says to the paralysed man: "Get up!"

GET UP!

The four men have overcome many difficulties to bring their paralysed friend to Jesus.

Jesus welcomes him. He says to the paralysed man, "My child, your sins are forgiven." These words surprise the crowd and the four men who were expecting to see their friend stand up. Jesus speaks and acts as the Son of God. But the scribes do not want to acknowledge this.

At once his words are fulfilled: the man stands up.

How powerful Jesus' word is! It's a word which saves and heals. In the same way, when Jesus says: "your sins are forgiven", he brings about wonderful healing, even though it is invisible. Jesus sets the man free from sin. By healing the man of his paralysis, Jesus invites the scribes and the whole crowd to believe that he is truly the Son of God.

MY CHILD, YOUR SINS ARE FORGIVEN

They all praised God!

Write down the sentences and draw in the boxes the healing of the paralysed man in the right order.

1	2	3
4	5	6

They all praised God.
"My child, your sins are forgiven."
The man got up and picked up his stretcher.
"Who can forgive sins, but God?"
"Pick up your stretcher and go off home."
Some people brought a paralysed man to him.

The word of God in my life

What does Jesus show us through this miracle?

....

....

....

The paralysed man's friends overcame all obstacles thanks to their great:

....

Find the hidden word which is in a diagonal line on the grid and colour the boxes to show it.

		C	R	O	W	D							
			O	P	P	O	S	I	T	I	O	N	
			U	N	B	E	L	I	E	F			
		R	O	O	F								
			S	C	R	I	B	E	S				
		F	O	R	B	I	D	D	E	N			
						D	E	S	P	A	I	R	
	H	O	P	E	L	E	S	S	N	E	S	S	
					T	E	A	C	H	E	R	S	
D	I	S	C	O	U	R	A	G	E	M	E	N	T

What Jesus has done for the paralysed man, he will do for each of us in

the .... of ....

Each evening I COMMIT MYSELF to asking Jesus to forgive my failures and to give him thanks for all the good things I have done with the help of his grace during the day.

I REMEMBER:

My child,
your sins are forgiven.
Get up and walk!

I also learn by heart a prayer asking for forgiveness and a prayer of praise.

I confess to almighty God
and to you, my brothers and sisters,
that I have greatly sinned,
in my thoughts and in my words,
in what I have done
and in what I have failed to do;
through my fault, through my fault,
through my most grievous fault;
therefore I ask blessed Mary ever-Virgin,
all the Angels and Saints,
and you, my brothers and sisters,
to pray for me to the Lord our God.

Glory to God in the highest,
and on earth peace to people of good will.

We praise you,
we bless you,
we adore you,
we glorify you,
we give you thanks for your great glory,
Lord God, heavenly King,
O God, almighty Father.

Lord Jesus Christ, Only Begotten Son,
Lord God, Lamb of God, Son of the Father,
You take away the sins of the world:
have mercy on us;
you take away the sins of the world,
receive our prayer;
You are seated at the right hand of the Father,
have mercy on us.

For you alone are the Holy One,
you alone are the Lord,
you alone are the Most High,
Jesus Christ,
with the Holy Spirit,
in the glory of God the Father.
Amen.

I sing

I'm trading my sorrows

I pray

Jesus, you know everything about me.
You can see what paralyses me,
what keeps me away from you.
You know my sin.
You know what you need to heal in me.
I need your forgiveness.

Jesus, you can also see my faith, my trust.
I believe in the power of your word.
I want to walk with you!

Jesus,
I would like you to say to me:
"Your sins are forgiven. Get up!"
Then I would run to you again.

Jesus,
give me the joy of being saved!
To you be praise and glory
forever and ever. Amen!

I AM THE GOOD SHEPHERD, I LAY DOWN MY LIFE FOR MY SHEEP

7. JESUS, THE GOOD SHEPHERD

The paschal mystery, source of forgiveness

THE WORD OF GOD

LUKE 15:1-7

[01] Tax collectors and sinners meanwhile, were all seeking [Jesus'] company to hear what he had to say, [02] and the Pharisees and the scribes complained, "This man", they said "welcomes sinners and eats with them." [03] So he spoke this parable to them:

[04] "What man among you with a hundred sheep, losing one, would not leave the ninety-nine in the wilderness, and go after the missing one till he found it? [05] And when he found it, would he not joyfully take it on his shoulders? [06] and then, when he got home, call together his friends and neighbours? 'Rejoice with me' he would say, 'I have found my sheep that was lost!'

[07] In the same way, I tell you, there will be more rejoicing in heaven over one repentant sinner, than over ninety-nine virtuous men who have no need of repentance."

JOHN 10:11-15. 28

[11] "I am the good shepherd: the good shepherd is one who lays down his life for his sheep. [12] The hired man, since he is not the shepherd, and the sheep do not belong to him, abandons the sheep and runs away as soon as he sees a wolf coming, and then the wolf attacks and scatters the sheep; [13] this is because he is only a hired man and has no concern for the sheep.

[14] I am the good shepherd; [15] [...] and I lay down my life for my sheep.

[...] [28] I give them eternal life; they will never be lost, and no one will ever steal them from me."

I welcome the word of God

The shepherd is Jesus. He has the same tender-hearted love as his Father: he does not want even one of his children to be lost. Jesus has come to search for the lost sheep. For him, each one of his sheep is unique.

The lost sheep represents the sinner who is searching for happiness far away from God. He or she wanders far away from the shepherd and the flock. God, in his goodness, sent Jesus to bring the lost sheep back.

The sheep who has been found is the sinner who has turned back to God and who is now sharing the happiness of the children of God. There is great rejoicing over this in heaven.

PARABLE OF THE LOST SHEEP

Jesus, the true shepherd, goes as far as risking his life to protect his sheep. He accepts death on the cross in order to save them. Jesus gives his own life for his sheep. But the shepherd who only looks after the sheep because he is being paid to do so, will not risk his life to save the sheep; he will abandon the sheep when he sees danger coming.

The wolf represents the devil. Jesus refers to him as the enemy of God, the one who wants to deceive, who brings division between Jesus' friends and wants to separate them from him. We should not be afraid of him because Jesus is more powerful than all the evil in the world. The sheep can place all their trust in him. Jesus said: "I give them eternal life; they will never be lost, and no one will ever

steal them from me." These words are filled with hope for those who believe in Jesus. The good shepherd gives eternal life to all those who follow him; he gives them life and happiness without end.

JESUS THE GOOD SHEPHERD GIVES ETERNAL LIFE

The word of God in my life

What does the good shepherd do for his sheep?

....

....

....

Write your own prayer which tells us of the joy of God's MERCY AND FORGIVENESS

M ....

E..

R..

C..

Y..

In my **prayer corner,** I place a crucifix which will remind me that Jesus gave his life for us.

I COMMIT MYSELF to giving thanks to Jesus often for his love and care for each one of us.

I REMEMBER:

There will be more rejoicing in heaven over one repentant sinner.

I sing

Thank you, Jesus, or another song suggested by your catechist.

I pray

in front of Jesus on the cross

O Jesus, good shepherd,
you have come to search for me.
Like the sheep, you carry me on your
    shoulders.
With you, I fear nothing, your hand guides me.
I walk in safety close to you.

O Jesus, good shepherd,
I look at you on the cross.
How great is your love for us!
How can I ever thank you enough?
You loved us so much that you died for us.

O Jesus, good shepherd,
I want to stay by the cross,
to receive the life that comes from you.
Make me holy. Make me pure.
Give me the joy of being saved!
May your risen life be my light!

RECEIVE THE HOLY SPIRIT.
THOSE WHOSE SINS YOU FORGIVE, THEY ARE FORGIVEN

8. THE PRIEST, SERVANT OF GOD'S MERCY

The priest, servant of God's mercy

THE WORD OF GOD

LUKE 6:12-19

[12] Now it was about this time that [Jesus] went out into the hills to pray; and he spent the whole night in prayer to God. [13] When day came, he summoned his disciples and picked out twelve of them; he called them "apostles": [14] Simon, whom he called Peter, and his brother Andrew; James, John, Philip, Bartholomew, [15] Matthew, Thomas, James son of Alpheus, Simon called the Zealot, [16] Judas son of James, and Judas Iscariot, who became a traitor.

[17] He then came down with them and stopped at a piece of level ground where there was a large gathering of his disciples with a great crowd of people from all parts of Judaea and from Jerusalem and from the coastal region of Tyre and Sidon [18] who had come to hear him and to be cured of their diseases. [19] People tormented by unclean spirits were also cured and everyone in the crowd was trying to touch him because power came out of him that cured them all.

JOHN 20:21-23

[21] [Jesus] said to them again, "Peace be with you! As the Father sent me, so am I sending you." [22] […] He breathed on them. and said, "Receive the Holy Spirit. [23] For those whose sins you forgive, they are forgiven; for those whose sins you retain, they are retained."

I welcome the word of God

Jesus prayed to the Father for a long time before choosing his apostles. He called the twelve to be with him and to continue his mission. Jesus takes them with him to meet all those who need him. They are all waiting for his word and some ask for healing. The apostles are witnesses of the goodness and mercy of their master.

JESUS PRAYS ALL NIGHT AND CHOOSES TWELVE APOSTLES

After Jesus' death and resurrection, when the disciples had locked themselves in the house out of fear, the risen Jesus shows himself to them. He comes to them with words filled with mercy. He says "Peace be with you!" and he breathes the Holy Spirit upon them.

Jesus understands their fear and does not rebuke them. He gives them his peace. Comforted by the words of the risen Christ, the apostles can hear his call once more: "I am sending you".

FOR THOSE WHOSE SINS YOU FORGIVE, THEY ARE FORGIVEN

By the gift of the Spirit, Jesus gives his apostles the power to forgive sins in his name. Continuing his mission, they now become the shepherds of the flock.

HE BREATHES THE SPIRIT UPON THEM

The word of God in my life

Jesus has given a mission to his apostles. With Jesus they now become the shepherds – the pastors – of his Church.

Can you find their names in this box?

The names "James" and "Judas" only appear once.

G	E	A	I	U	J	B	E	B	R	L	K	P	S	M
L	W	O	T	F	E	T	B	T	Z	G	I	T	I	H
L	T	J	Z	U	S	U	I	J	O	L	W	Z	M	I
M	T	S	E	S	U	M	W	O	I	V	S	I	O	F
J	A	M	E	S	S	W	Q	H	S	A	N	L	N	E
H	V	T	A	Z	G	U	P	N	M	T	C	H	R	Z
K	F	X	T	J	B	F	M	O	X	O	Y	R	J	L
H	X	V	R	H	E	K	H	P	A	G	B	J	G	L
L	S	D	K	W	E	T	N	U	N	X	S	U	T	I
H	A	N	V	P	X	W	F	N	D	L	O	D	Z	X
R	A	D	C	E	X	D	L	A	R	Z	F	A	I	N
B	Z	W	N	T	G	G	W	P	E	U	C	S	V	U
S	J	M	R	E	V	M	M	N	W	F	C	V	U	L
M	S	K	O	R	R	M	B	O	S	X	C	T	C	K
Y	Y	B	A	R	T	H	O	L	O	M	E	W	J	N

....

....

....

....

Priests have the responsibility of announcing the Gospel to everyone, to be the pastors of the Christian community and to pass on the life of the risen Jesus through the sacraments. They continue the mission given by Jesus to his apostles.

When I go and meet the priest to receive the sacrament of reconciliation, I will talk to him as I would talk to Jesus himself. I will tell him my sins. I will be forgiven, reconciled with God and with others. Jesus will do for me what he has done for so many people: he will raise me up and fill me with his mercy.

Colour these words:

Receive the
Holy Spirit;
for those
whose sins you
forgive, they
are forgiven.

What is a priest? What do priests do?

....

....

....

Write down the names of the priests you know.

....

....

....

Write down the words that the priest will say to you, in the name of Jesus.

"I ....

....

....

I COMMIT MYSELF to going with trust to the priest to receive forgiveness of my sins

I REMEMBER:

Through the gift of the Holy Spirit, Jesus passes on to the apostles and to the priests the power to forgive sins in his name.

I sing

The Lord's my shepherd,
I'll not want

I pray

Jesus, you have chosen priests for us.
They are shepherds for us.
In your name, they heal and forgive.
Through them, you continue to save us.

Jesus, soon I will receive your forgiveness
in the sacrament of reconciliation.
I know and I believe
that the word of the priest is your word.
When the priest says to me:
"I absolve you from your sins",
it is you, Jesus, who will forgive me.

Thank you, Jesus:
you are always with us.
Thank you for making me new
through your forgiveness.
Thank you for giving us priests.

9. MY CONSCIENCE, A GUIDE FOR MY LIFE

My conscience, a guide in the depths of my heart

THE WORD OF GOD

MATTHEW 6:1-6. 16-18

01 Be careful not to parade your good deeds before men to attract their notice; by doing this you will lose all reward from your Father in heaven.

02 So when you give alms, do not have it trumpeted before you; this is what the hypocrites do in the synagogues and in the streets to win men's admiration. I tell you solemnly, they have had their reward.

03 But when you give alms, your left hand must not know what your right is doing; 04 your almsgiving must be secret, and your Father who sees all that is done in secret will reward you.

05 And when you pray, do not imitate the hypocrites: they love to say their prayers standing up in the synagogues and at the street corners for people to see them. I tell you solemnly, they have had their reward. 06 But when you pray, go to your private room and, when you have shut your door, pray to your Father who is in that secret place, and your Father who sees all that is done in secret will reward you.

[…] 16 When you fast, do not put on a gloomy look, as the hypocrites do: they pull long faces to let men know they are fasting. I tell you solemnly: they have had their reward.

17 But when you fast, put oil on your head and wash your face, so that no one will know you are fasting 18 except your Father, who sees all that is done in secret; and your Father, who sees all that is done in secret will reward you.

I welcome the word of God

When Jesus was teaching, he often asked his listeners to reflect on the way they lived and acted.

Jesus presents to us three good actions. **Write them down:**

....

....

....

These three actions can be inspired either by a good or by a bad intention.

✎Look carefully at the Gospel text and, in a small group, discuss the way Jesus repeats certain things. Then write down:

Attitudes Jesus condemns	Attitudes Jesus encourages
....	....
....	....
....	....
....	....

Jesus shows us the right attitude: "When you give alms... when you pray... when you fast... **do it in secret.**" For your actions to be good, they must be done out of love. The measure of love is personal, we give according to our own heart, and it is secret: God sees in secret and will reward us.

The word of God in my life

Carefully read the text below, then try and discover what, in the secret depths of our heart, helps us distinguish the good to be done from the evil to be avoided.

Read down in a diagonal line to find the word.

LIKE A FRIENDLY VOI**C**E

OPEN TO GOD,

OF GOOD AND JUST COUNSEL

IN THE MOST SECRET PART OF MY HEART

YOU HELP ME CHOOSE TO LOVE

IN FREEDOM

PEACEFUL LIGHT,

WHICH PRAISES,QUESTIONS,

EDUCATES, WARNS, ENCOURAGES

IN THE SECRET OF MY HEART

....

I learn to enter deep inside my own heart, in the secret place of my conscience, where I choose and decide. I learn to listen to the Holy Spirit.
At night, before I fall asleep, I find Jesus in prayer.
I look back over my day in the light of the Gospel:
"Jesus,

– have I loved God with my whole heart, by being faithful to prayer time, like you did?
– have I loved other people as you love them, by sharing with them and listening to them?
– have I tried to please God by obeying his word?"

I COMMIT MYSELF to reflecting each night on my day, to give thanks to Jesus and to ask for his forgiveness.

I should have helped him and I didn't do it!

Jesus, what do you want me to do?

Thank you for giving me the courage to forgive!

I REMEMBER:

When you give to others... when you pray...
when you fast... do it in secret.
Your Father who sees all that is done in secret
will reward you.

I pray

with the psalms

My God, listen to my prayer.
Give me your light.
Help me to discover where I fail to love.
Teach me your ways,
so that I may walk in faithfulness to you.

My God, have mercy on me,
in your great tenderness look at me.
You know my sin,
even if it is hidden.

You know the intentions of my heart.
You know that I want to do what is good,
but that I often do what is not pleasing to you.
Give me courage to do what is right.

My God, wash away my sins and purify me.
Place your truth in the depth of my heart.

I trust in you, my God.
I know that you never abandon me.
When I fall, I cry out to you
and you rescue me.
I thank you with all my heart
because your love for me is so great.

I sing

Listen, listen, your conscience speaks to you

10. THE PARABLE OF MERCY

The son comes back to his father

THE WORD OF GOD

LUKE 15:11-19

[11] [Jesus] also said, "A man had two sons. [12] The younger said to his father, 'Father, let me have the share of the estate that would come to me.' So the father divided the property between them. [13] A few days later, the younger son got together everything he had and left for a distant country, where he squandered his money on a life of debauchery.

[14] When he had spent it all, that country experienced a severe famine, and now he began to feel the pinch, [15] so he hired himself out to one of the local inhabitants, who put him on his farm to feed the pigs. [16] And he would willingly have filled his belly with the husks the pigs were eating, but no one offered him anything.

[17] Then he came to his senses and said, 'How many of my father's paid servants have more food than they want, and here am I dying of hunger! [18] I will leave this place and go to my father and say, Father, I have sinned against heaven and against you. [19] I no longer deserve to be called your son. Treat me as one of your paid servants.'

..../....

I welcome the word of God

Write down the relevant part of the story under each picture.

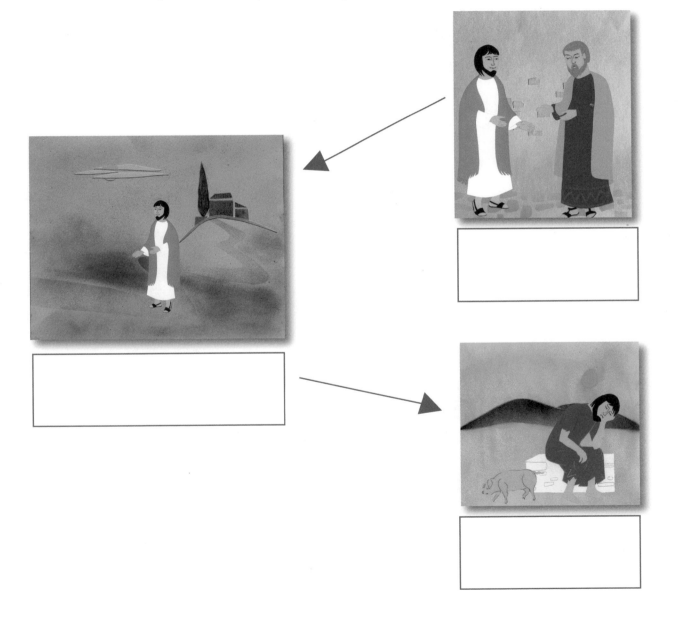

..../....

LUKE 15:20-24

[20] So he left the place and went back to his father. While he was still a long way off, his father saw him and was moved with pity. He ran to the boy, clasped him in his arms and kissed him tenderly. [21] Then his son said, 'Father, I have sinned against heaven and against you. I no longer deserve to be called your son.'

[22] But the father said to his servants: 'Quick!' Bring out the best robe and put it on him; put a ring on his finger and sandals on his feet. [23] Bring the calf we have been fattening and kill it; we are going to have a feast, a celebration, [24] because this son of mine was dead, and has come back to life; he was lost, and is found!' And they began to celebrate.

The word of God in my life

Who is this Father, so full of forgiveness?

....

Who does this young, thoughtless and selfish son represent?

....

What do you think the inheritance received from the father might mean for us?

....

What does this parable teach us about the effects of sin?

....

....

....

What does this parable tell us about the heart of God?

....

....

....

Begin to discover who God is using the grid.

A₁	B₂	C₃	D₄	E₅	F₆	G₇	H₈	I₉	J₁₀	K₁₁	L₁₂	M₁₃
N₁₄	O₁₅	P₁₆	Q₁₇	R₁₈	S₁₉	T₂₀	U₂₁	V₂₂	W₂₃	X₂₄	Y₂₅	Z₂₆

| 20 | 8 | 5 | | 8 | 5 | 1 | 18 | 20 | | 15 | 6 | | 7 | 15 | 4 |

| 9 | 19 | | 6 | 21 | 12 | 12 | | 15 | 6 | | 13 | 5 | 18 | 3 | 25 |

God's heart is full of forgiveness and mercy. It is more tender than the love a mother has in her heart for her children. God our Father is filled with joy when he sees us come back to him and wants to celebrate!

I COMMIT MYSELF to forgiving others so that I may prepare myself well to receive the sacrament of reconciliation.

I REMEMBER: act of contrition.

This prayer will help me to say how sorry I am for my sins and how much I want never to sin again.

> O my God, because you are so good,
> I am very sorry that I have sinned against you,
> and by the help of your grace,
> I will not sin again. Amen.

I pray

Father, you know that, like this son,
I sometimes distance myself from you.
Your tenderness is without measure
You never stop waiting for me to come back
    to you.

Father, I do not want to stay far from you.
I run into your arms,
which are always open for me. You wait
    patiently for me.

Father, I am not afraid.
I trust in your love.
I know that your love is stronger than my sin
Your love for me is beyond my imagination!

Jesus, I thank you
for having made known to me
the love of the Father,
for having revealed to me his infinite
    tenderness, and his mercy!

I sing

We have a Father

I WILL GET UP AND GO BACK TO MY FATHER

11. CELEBRATION OF RECONCILIATION

Celebration of the sacrament of reconciliation

Celebrating the sacrament of reconciliation

He came to his senses

Examination of conscience

I call on the Holy Spirit, to help me to look at my life in the light of the parable of the son who comes back to his father. I reflect in silence on my actions, my attitudes, and my intentions. That is what is called an **examination of conscience**. There are many good and beautiful actions in my everyday life. There are also actions and words which I regret: when I forget God or when I hurt others... What things in my life, what actions of mine, need the forgiveness of Jesus?

I will get up and go
to my father

Contrition

I let myself be guided by the great love that the Father has for each one of us. I look at Jesus on the cross, at his great love for us and his suffering for us. This look of love helps me to truly regret my failures to love and brings my heart to real **contrition**. Jesus calls me to **conversion**.

Confession

"O my God, because you are so good,
I am very sorry that I have sinned against you,
and by the help of your grace,
I will not sin again. Amen."

Father, I have sinned

His father ran to
embrace him

Absolution

Now, the priest prays over me while he holds out his hands over me: "God, the Father of mercies, through the death and resurrection of his Son has reconciled the world to himself and sent the Holy Spirit among us for the forgiveness of sins; through the ministry of the Church may God give you pardon and peace."

Then he makes the sign of the cross, saying:

"And I absolve you from your sins in the name of the Father, and of the Son, and of the Holy Spirit. Go in peace!"

I also make the sign of the cross. I answer "Amen". At this moment, I receive the forgiveness of all my sins: **absolution**.

God renews in me the grace of my baptism.

I not longer deserve to
be called your child

Penance

To make up for the wrong things I have done, the priest gives me a **penance** (prayer, task or sacrifice). In reality, only Jesus can save us, by offering his life on the cross. Through my penance, I make the decision to respond better to the love of God and others. Conversion will be the work of a lifetime: it will be achieved by the grace of God and by my small efforts each day. Coming back to my place, I give thanks to Jesus for his forgiveness and I say or do my penance.

My child has come
back to life

The forgiveness I receive renews me in my dignity as a child of God. I thank him because...

- he has clothed me with the most beautiful robe: The grace of my baptism is renewed.
- he has put a ring on my finger: I am restored to my dignity as his child.
- he has put sandals on my feet: Now I can walk in the footsteps of Jesus.

Let us celebrate and have a feast!

The light, the joy and the peace of Jesus are in me, and I can now share in the banquet of the Eucharist by receiving Jesus, the Bread of Life.

With the son of the parable
I acknowledge that I am a sinner

I COMMIT MYSELF to receiving the sacrament
of reconciliation and to preparing myself well, so
that I may experience the great feasts of the Church
meaningfully.

I REMEMBER the parts of the sacrament of
reconciliation. This will help me to receive it in the
best way and to benefit from it.

Examination of conscience
Contrition
Confession
Absolution
Penance
Thanksgiving

Now I give thanks to God

I sing

What can I give to you

I pray

Thank you, Father,
you clothe me with the white garment,
you invite me to sit
at the family table, as your child.
How could I have imagined
such love, such forgiveness!

Thank you, Father,
you put a ring back on my finger,
a sign of your renewed covenant.
You are the faithful God,
who always trusts us.
How could I have imagined
such love, such forgiveness!

Thank you, Father,
you put sandals on my feet,
you tell me again: "Get up and walk."
You give me the strength of the Holy Spirit
to walk according to your will.
How could I have imagined
such love, such forgiveness!

I received the sacrament of reconciliation

on the   /   /

Thank you Jesus for your forgiveness!

My heart is filled with joy!

The journey towards the sacrament of the Eucharist

I prepare my heart
to receive and welcome Jesus,
Bread of Life

THE SOWER SOWS THE WORD

1. JESUS, WORD OF LIFE

I receive and welcome Jesus, the Word of life

THE WORD OF GOD

MARK 4:1-14. 20

[01] Again, [Jesus] began to teach by the lakeside; but such a huge crowd gathered round him, that he got into a boat on the lake and sat there. The people were all along the shore, at the water's edge [02] He taught them many things in parables, and in the course of his teaching he said to them,

[03] "Listen! Imagine a sower going out to sow. [04] Now it happened that as he sowed, some of the seed fell on the edge of the path; and the birds came and ate it up. [05] Some seed fell on rocky ground, where it found little soil and sprang up straight away, because there was no depth of earth; [06] and when the sun came it was scorched and, not having any roots, it withered away. [07] Some seed fell into thorns; and the thorns grew up and choked it; and it produced no crop. [08] And some seeds fell into rich soil and, growing tall and strong produced crop; and yielded thirty, sixty, even a hundredfold." [09] And he said, "Listen, anyone who has ears to hear."

[10] When he was alone, the Twelve, together with the others who formed his company, asked what the parables meant. [...]. [13] Jesus said to them, "Do you not understand this parable? [...]

[14] What the sower is sowing is the word. [...]. [20] And there are those who have received the seed in rich soil. They hear the word and accept it and yield a harvest, thirty, and sixty and a hundredfold."

I welcome the word of God

Jesus spends long hours teaching. Crowds gather around him because people love to hear his word. Jesus uses the language of parables to gain the attention of his audience. By using these images, Jesus helps them to discover the hidden realities of the kingdom of God.

He tells them to: "Listen!"

LISTEN!

Jesus is the Word that comes from God; he is the Master who teaches with kindness and authority. Jesus knows the human heart is easily distracted and restless. He wants all our hearts to be open to receive his love, because he is the Saviour.

The seed is the word of God. Jesus is the sower. He scatters his word generously. This word is given to everyone. No one is left out. The word of God falls into every heart, into very different types of soil. It touches each one in their personal history, their personality, attitudes, qualities and shortcomings.

The edge of the path, the rocky ground and the thorns describe the difficulties many people have in receiving the word. The good soil represents those who welcome the word with an open and generous heart.

The word of God has an extraordinary life-giving power. It produces fruit in abundance. The word of God transforms the person who listens to it and keeps it. It makes that person a true disciple, someone who loves and acts like Jesus.

THE SOWER WENT OUT TO SOW

The word of God in my life

The different soils in the parable of the sower

When is my heart like the edge of the path?

....

What does the rocky ground represent?

....

What could the thorns which choke the word be?

....

How can we be the good soil that welcomes the word of God?

....

I write down the capital letter at the beginning of each sentence and decorate it beautifully.

☐ et your mind be open!

☐ nvite the Holy Spirit in you!

☐ et your heart on the essential!

☐ urn your eyes to Jesus!

☐ nter into his friendship!

☐ ourish yourself with his word!

I have discovered a very important word, mentioned by Jesus in the parable. **I write it down here.**

I COMMIT MYSELF to preparing for my first Holy Communion by listening even better in catechesis or at Mass. I colour one ear of wheat each time I am attentive to the word of God.

I REMEMBER

Those who receive the seed in rich soil, hear the word and accept it and yield a harvest.

I sing

Jesus told this parable of a farmer sowing seed

I pray

Jesus,
my soul is thirsting for your word.
Your word reveals to me
the secrets of your kingdom.
It is a light for my life.
It guides me along the right path.
Help me love your word.
Help me live according to your word.
Help me to put it into practice.

Holy Spirit,
make my heart ready to listen to Jesus,
the Word of Life.

Mary, you who welcomed and pondered the word of God,
help me to keep it,
with an attentive and obedient heart.
Like you, I want to nourish my heart with the word of God
so that I may bear fruit in plenty.

THEY ATE AND WERE FILLED

2. JESUS MULTIPLIES THE BREAD

The multiplication of the loaves

THE WORD OF GOD

MARK 6:30-46

30 The apostles rejoined Jesus and told him all they had done and taught. 31 Then he said to them, "You must come away to some lonely place all by yourselves and rest for a while." For there were so many coming and going that the apostles had no time even to eat. 32 So they went off in a boat to a lonely place where they could be by themselves. 33 But people saw them going, and many could guess where; and from every town, they all hurried to the place on foot and reached it before them. 34 So as he stepped ashore, he saw a large crowd, and he took pity on them, because they were like sheep without a shepherd, and he set himself to teach them at some length.

35 By now it was getting very late, and his disciples came up to him and said, "This is a lonely place and it is getting very late, 36 so send them away, and they can go to the farms and villages round about, to buy themselves something to eat." 37 He replied, "Give them something to eat yourselves." They answered, "Are we to go and spend two hundred denarii on bread for them to eat?" 38 "How many loaves have you?" he asked "Go and see." And when they had found out they said, "Five, and two fish." 39 Then he ordered them to get all the people together in groups on the green grass, 40 and they sat down on the ground in squares of hundreds and fifties. 41 Then he took the five loaves and the two fish, raised his eyes to heaven and said the blessing; then he broke the loaves, and handed them to his disciples to distribute among the people. He also shared out the two fish among them all.

42 They all ate as much as they wanted. 43 They collected twelve basketfuls of scraps of bread and pieces of fish. 44 Those who had eaten the loaves numbered five thousand men. 45 Directly after this, he made his disciples get into the boat and go on ahead to Bethsaida, while he himself sent the crowd away. 46 After saying goodbye to them, he went off into the hills to pray.

I welcome the word of God

The disciples return from their mission. They tell Jesus everything they did. Jesus listens to them and invites them to come away from the crowd and go into a lonely place. But Jesus and his disciples are quickly joined by a crowd of people who are waiting for them!

Jesus looks around at all these people.
He is moved with compassion for them in the depths of his heart. Jesus takes pity on them. He tells them all about the love of the Father and the kingdom of Heaven. He comforts them and raises their spirits.

HE TOOK PITY ON THEM

GIVE THEM SOMETHING TO EAT YOURSELVES

THEY GATHERED UP THE LOAVES THAT WERE LEFT

Time goes by. No one is tired of listening to Jesus. It is late and it would be sensible to send the people home now because they have nothing to eat.

JESUS WENT OFF INTO THE HILLS TO PRAY

This lack of food will be an opportunity for Jesus to show his love. He raises his eyes to heaven. Jesus prays to his Father, as he always does. Giving thanks, he presents the loaves and fish to the Father. He breaks the bread, gives the loaves and fish to his disciples and asks them to distribute them to the crowd.

With only five loaves and two fish, Jesus feeds the whole crowd. They all ate what they wanted. By multiplying the loaves, Jesus demonstrates both his love for all people and his power as the Son of God.

Twelve baskets full of scraps are collected. The disciples and all those who have eaten are filled with wonder! The love of Jesus is infinite, like the love of his Father. He gives in abundance, surpassing all human measures, because he is God.

People are amazed by such a miracle. However, Jesus does not look for praise from the crowd, but sends them away. He withdraws into the silence of the hills to be with his Father in prayer.

The word of God in my life

Why does Jesus tell his disciples to go away to a lonely place?

....

Why is Jesus moved with compassion for the people?

....

Where have you heard before words that are similar to the Gospel below?

....

… and, raising his eyes to heaven, he said the blessing and
broke the bread and gave it…

....

Number the sentences in the correct order to match the Gospel:

❏ They all ate as much as they wanted.

❏ Jesus took pity on them.

❏ Jesus went off into the hills to pray.

❏ He set himself to teach them at some length.

❏ "Give them something to eat yourselves."

❏ "Come away to some lonely place… and rest."

I DECIDE what kind of "loaves" I want to offer Jesus:

....

....

Write down a prayer of thanksgiving and praise on the cut out shape of a loaf of bread which you can place below.

I REMEMBER

The miracles of Jesus are signs which show the power of God's love.
By his miracles, Jesus shows that he is the Messiah, sent by the Father. Miracles strengthen our faith in Jesus our Saviour.

I sing

All that I am, all that I do

I pray

Thank you, Jesus, for all that you do!
You love us,
you tell us about the Father,
you take special care of us.
Like the crowd who followed you, we are filled with wonder
at the signs you give us.

I know, Jesus,
that you really are the Son of God,
you are the Almighty.
With only five loaves
you fed a great crowd.
Jesus, I believe you can do anything.

Jesus, you want me to help you,
you want me to share
the good things you have given me
and the love that comes from you.
Like the child,
I want to offer you everything I have.
It's almost nothing...
but you can do great things with it.

I AM THE BREAD OF LIFE

3. JESUS ANNOUNCES THE EUCHARIST

Revealing the mystery of the Eucharist

THE WORD OF GOD

JOHN 6:22-69

²² Next day, the crowd that had stayed on the other side saw [...] ²⁴ that neither Jesus nor his disciples were there, they got into those boats and crossed to Capernaum to look for Jesus. ²⁵ When they found him on the other side, they said to him, "Rabbi, when did you come here?" ²⁶ Jesus answered, "[...] you are not looking for me because you have seen the signs but because you had all the bread you wanted to eat. ²⁷ Do not work for food that cannot last, but work for food that endures to eternal life.[...] " ²⁸ Then they said to him, "What must we do if we are to do the works that God wants?" ²⁹ Jesus gave them this answer, "This is working for God: you must believe in the one he has sent." ³⁰ So they said, "What sign will you give to show us that we should believe in you? What work will you do? ³¹ Our fathers had manna to eat in the desert [...]" ³² Jesus answered, "[...] it was not Moses who gave you bread from heaven, it is my Father who gives you the bread from heaven, the true bread; ³³ for the bread of God is that which comes down from heaven and gives life to the world." ³⁴ "Sir", they said, "Give us that bread always." ³⁵ Jesus answered, "I am the bread of life. He who comes to me will never be hungry; he who believes in me will never thirst." [...] ⁴¹ Meanwhile the Jews were complaining to each other about him because he had said, "I am the bread that came down from heaven." ⁴² "Surely, this is Jesus son of Joseph" they said. "We know his father and mother. "[...]" ⁴⁷ I tell you most solemnly, everybody who believes has eternal life. [...] ⁴⁹ Your fathers ate the manna in the desert and they are dead. [...] ⁵¹ I am the living bread which has come down from heaven. Anyone who eats this bread will live for ever; and the bread that I shall give is my flesh, for the life of the world." ⁵² Then the Jews started arguing with one another, "How can this man give us his flesh to eat?" they said. Jesus replied [...] ⁵⁴ "Anyone who does eat my flesh and drink my blood has eternal life, and I shall raise him up on the last day." [...] ⁶⁶ After this many of his disciples left him and stopped going with him. ⁶⁷ Then Jesus said to the Twelve, "What about you, do you want to go away too?" ⁶⁸ Simon Peter answered, "Lord, who shall we go to? You have the message of eternal life, ⁶⁹ and we believe; we know that you are the Holy One of God."

I welcome the word of God

The day after the miracle of the multiplication of the loaves, Jesus sees the crowd looking for him again. They want to be fed once more.

While the people around him continue to think about physical bread to feed their bodily hunger, Jesus invites them to believe in him, in order to do the work of God. He tries to help them discover a more important food: the bread of eternal life. This is the true food that can satisfy them, by feeding their souls. Jesus reveals that he himself is this bread which has come down from heaven.

I AM THE BREAD OF LIFE

Some think that Jesus is merely their neighbour from Nazareth, the carpenter's son. They do not recognise him as the Son of God.

Through this pronouncement on the Bread of Life, Jesus challenges his listeners to make a choice. He calls them to take a further step in faith and trust. Not only does he say to them that he comes from heaven and that he is the living bread, but he also promises eternal life to those who eat this bread!

The words of Jesus are mysterious. They astonish and shock his listeners. This revelation of the Bread of Life invites them to choose to believe in Jesus and commit themselves to following him. However, many walk away.

WE BELIEVE!

The question Jesus asks: "Do you want to go away too?" gives the apostles an opportunity to choose him once more and to acknowledge him as Lord. On behalf of the twelve, Peter affirms his faith: "We believe!" They remain with him and continue to accompany him.

The word of God in my life

How can you "do the work of God"?

....

Find nine words that you heard during this session hidden in the grid. Write them down below.

B	E	L	I	E	V	E	Q	T	X	H
M	W	I	W	H	O	C	R	L	J	E
Z	I	H	Q	R	T	U	P	B	F	A
X	E	R	Y	K	S	I	U	K	T	V
Y	I	P	A	T	C	G	A	A	D	E
F	O	O	D	C	Y	Q	D	F	I	N
Z	W	Q	J	O	L	K	Q	N	Y	J
D	A	E	R	B	Q	E	G	N	K	E
W	L	F	B	X	C	I	G	T	R	D
A	U	I	R	I	S	H	U	O	A	E
H	T	L	R	V	B	O	W	N	F	S

....

....

Write a sentence with these words:

....

....

I DECIDE MYSELF this week, to pray to Jesus saying:

Jesus, I believe, you are the Bread of Life.

I colour the sentence above

I REMEMBER

Everybody who believes in Jesus has eternal life.
I need his word, I need the Bread of Life to strengthen my life
as a child of God.

I sing

Bread of Life, truth eternal

I pray

Jesus, you said:
"I am the bread which gives LIFE!"

Your words are too great for me,
they are so mysterious!
But I believe you can do all things!
I believe in your words,
I trust in you.
What you say, you always do.

Give me the bread of your word!
Give me the bread of your body!
I hunger for you, Jesus!
"To whom shall we go?
You have the words of eternal life!"

Jesus, I love you,
I want to follow you,
I want to live with your life,
now and always.

THIS IS MY BODY, THIS IS MY BLOOD

4. JESUS GIVES HIMSELF AT THE LAST SUPPER

The gift of the Eucharist

THE WORD OF GOD

MATTHEW 26:17-20. 26-32

[17] Now on the first day of Unleavened Bread, the disciples came to Jesus to say, "Where do you want us to make the preparations for you to eat the Passover?" [18] "Go to so-and-so in the city" he replied "and say to him, 'The Master says: My time is near. It is at your house that I am keeping Passover with my disciples.'" [19] The disciples did what Jesus told them and prepared the Passover.

[20] When evening came he was at table with the twelve disciples.[...] [26] Now as they were eating, Jesus took some bread, and when he had said the blessing he broke it, and gave it to the disciples. "Take it and eat;" he said " this is my body." [27] Then he took a cup, and when he had returned thanks, he gave it to them. "Drink all of you from this," he said [28] "for this is my blood, the blood of the covenant, which is to be poured out for many for the forgiveness of sins. [29] From now on, I tell you, I shall not drink wine until the day I drink the new wine with you in the kingdom of my Father."

[30] After psalms had been sung they left for the Mount of Olives. [31] Then Jesus said to them, "You will all lose faith in me this night, for the scripture says: I shall strike the shepherd and the sheep of the flock will be scattered, [32] but after my resurrection I shall go before you to Galilee."

I welcome the word of God

The Jewish Passover recalled the wonders that God had done to free his people from slavery in the land of Egypt. Today, the Passover is still a great feast for the Jewish people. Jesus chose

THE LAST SUPPER

this feast to celebrate his last supper with his disciples. His time, the moment of his death, is near. The leaders of the people, who do not believe in him, have decided to put him to death. Jesus is the true lamb, who gives his life to save us all from sin.

During his last supper with the twelve, Jesus fulfills the promise of the Bread of Life: he gives himself as food. Jesus says the blessing,

THE CROSS

and gives thanks. The apostles receive the bread that Jesus has just broken: this is his body. They receive the cup that Jesus gives them: this is his blood. They receive the Body and Blood of Christ in Holy Communion. The disciples are one with him.

Once the meal is over, Jesus and his apostles go to the Mount of Olives where Jesus loved to withdraw and pray. There, Jesus is arrested and Judas hands him over to the soldiers. The disciples all run away and leave Jesus alone.

Jesus allows himself to be led to the cross. He had broken the bread. Now his body is handed over to be broken. He had offered the cup

THE RESURRECTION

of wine. Now his blood is poured out, offered for everyone, the blood of the new covenant for the forgiveness of sins.

Three days after his death, Jesus comes out of the tomb alive. The apostles find it difficult to believe in his resurrection. Jesus appears to them several times. He shows them his wounds, which they can touch. He eats with them. In this way, Jesus strengthens their faith: he is truly there, alive. His body is filled with life and glory. The twelve are comforted and strengthened by Jesus, risen and present among them. The promise is fulfilled: "Anyone who eats this bread will live forever and I will raise him up on the last day."

The word of God in my life

Each year, during Holy Week, we remember the paschal mystery of Jesus.
What do we celebrate on each of these days?

Maundy Thursday : ....

Good Friday : ....

Easter Sunday : ....

Draw a picture depicting each of the three days of the paschal mystery:

	Good Friday	
Maundy Thursday		Easter Sunday

Why is each Mass an Easter celebration?

....

....

....

Complete the sentences below with the following words:

"bread", "treasure", "Jesus", "wine", "eternal life", and "food".

The Eucharist is a .... because it gives us .... hidden under the

signs of .... and .... Jesus is our ....

He gives us ....

I DECIDE MYSELF to being more attentive during the Sunday Eucharist.

I REMEMBER

It is through faith that we recognise,
in this bread and wine,
the presence of God our master,
the risen Lord Jesus.

I sing

O Bread of Heaven, beneath this veil

I pray

"This is my body, this is my blood."
What a mystery!
Jesus, you are the bread
that comes from heaven!

This life-giving bread
is your body, Jesus,
this I believe.

When I look at you on the cross,
I am filled with wonder at your love.
You have given everything for us.
I love you, Jesus!

I want to come close to you.
When you come to me,
You will teach me how to love
as you love.

Jesus, give me your risen life!
I want to receive you, Jesus.
I long to receive you in Holy Communion.
I want to receive my life from you always!

DO THIS IN MEMORY OF ME

5. THE PASSING ON OF THE EUCHARIST

The passing on of the Eucharist

THE WORD OF GOD

FIRST LETTER OF SAINT PAUL TO THE CORINTHIANS 11:23-26

23 For this is what I received from the Lord, and in turn passed on to you: that on the same night that he was betrayed, the Lord Jesus took some bread, and 24 thanked God for it and broke it, and he said, "This is my body which is for you; do this as a memorial of me." 25 In the same way he took the cup after supper, and said, "This cup is the new covenant in my blood. Whenever you drink it, do this as a memorial of me." 26 Until the Lord comes, therefore, every time you eat this bread and drink this cup, you are proclaiming his death.

ACT OF THE APOSTLES 2:42. 46

42 These remained faithful to the teaching of the apostles, to the brotherhood, to the breaking of bread and to the prayers.
46 They went as a body to the Temple every day but met in their houses for the breaking of bread; they shared their food gladly and generously.

I welcome the word of God

Paul was a devout Jew who fought for the rights of God. As Paul was persecuting the first Christians, the risen Jesus made himself known to him. Jesus chose Paul so that he could also proclaim the Gospel. Paul became an apostle, like Peter and the others. He was not present at the Last Supper, so the apostles told him what Jesus had done on the evening of Maundy Thursday. In his turn, Paul passes on the tradition of the Eucharist to all those he evangelises.

"Do this in memory of me." Jesus gives his apostles the power and the mission to renew what he did during the Last Supper.

DO THIS IN MEMORY OF ME

Those who believe in Jesus and have received baptism begin to form the first Christian communities. They remain "faithful to the teaching of the apostles". They meet together regularly.

They live by the new commandment given by Jesus: "love one another as I have loved you." Their master had humbled himself by washing the feet of the twelve. Now they follow his example of service and charity in the "common life of sharing".

The apostles renew the action of "the breaking of the bread" which Jesus did before he died. The believers gather on Sundays and share in the Lord's Supper by receiving the Body and Blood of Christ in Communion.

They are faithful to "the prayers" and to the singing of the psalms both in the Temple and in their homes.

Their gatherings make real the joy of the Resurrection and the support of the whole Christian community.

BELIEVERS REMAINED FAITHFUL TO THE TEACHING OF THE APOSTLES, TO THE COMMON LIFE OF SHARING (COMMUNITY), TO THE BREAKING OF BREAD AND TO THE PRAYERS

The word of God in my life

Find the words hidden in the chalice:

 * Holy Communion
 * life without end
 * Jesus broke it
 * Jesus blessed and gave it to his disciples
 * word that goes with the verb "to give"
 * Those who receive are in C............... with Jesus

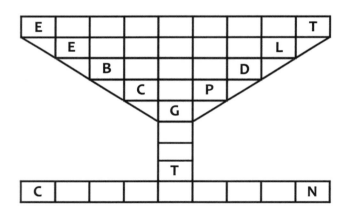

Using these hidden words, I write a short paragraph:

....

....

How did the first Christians refer to the Eucharist?

....

Who was Saint Paul?

....

....

Place in chronological order, in the arrows, the succession of those who have handed on the Eucharist to us: the first Christians, Jesus, our parish community, the apostles, the Church through the centuries.

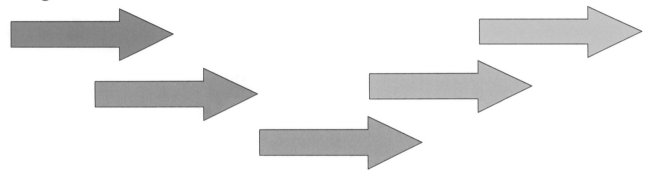

I DECIDE to participate in the Eucharist every Sunday.
In this way, I will live in Jesus and I will be a witness to others of his love.

I REMEMBER

Christians remain faithful to the
teaching of the apostles, to the
common life of sharing, to the
breaking of bread and to the prayers.

I pray

Jesus, you said to your disciples:
"Do this in memory of me".
Since that day, thanks to your priests,
the Eucharist is celebrated
everywhere throughout the world.

Thank you for so, so many
Eucharistic celebrations
where you continue to give yourself!

Each Sunday, you invite us
and you gather us as Church.
You teach us through your word
you give us a share in the Bread of Life.

Jesus,
give me enough love to remain faithful
to our meeting, each Sunday,
with all the people of my parish.
Give us one heart in praising you!

I sing

Oh, how could it be
that my God would welcome me into this
mystery.

BEHOLD THE DWELLING-PLACE OF GOD AMONG US

6. THE PEOPLE OF GOD CELEBRATE

The space where we celebrate

THE WORD OF GOD

REVELATION 21:3

03 "Then I heard a loud voice call from the throne, 'You see this city? Here God lives among men: He will make his home among them; they shall be his people, and he will be their God.'"

REVELATION 7:9- 15

09 I saw a huge number, impossible to count, of people from every nation, race, tribe and language; they were standing in front of the throne, and in front of the Lamb, dressed in white robes and holding palms in their hands. 12 They shouted aloud [....], "Amen! Praise and glory and wisdom and thanksgiving and honour and power and strength to our God for ever and ever. Amen!"[…] 15 […] They […] serve him, day and night, in his sanctuary.

I welcome the word of God

Glory

Praise   Wisdom

Honour   Power

Thanksgiving

Strength to our God

Saint John reveals to the first Christians what God made known to him in a vision. God showed him heaven, the kingdom to come. The throne is a symbol of the kingship of God, of his unique greatness. "The dwelling of God" is heaven, where God welcomes all people. Saint John saw a huge crowd from every nation. These are the saints. They stand before the throne and praise God. They wear a white garment, a symbol of baptism and of the light of the risen Lord. They praise Jesus, the Lamb of God, with palms, signs of their victory. The citizens of heaven have triumphed over evil thanks to the lamb who gave his life for them. They are so filled with happiness in the presence of the risen Lord, that they cannot find enough words of praise and thanksgiving!

BEHOLD THE DWELLING PLACE OF GOD AMONG US

On earth, God is present in our midst each time we gather together to praise him.

A GREAT CROWD FROM EVERY NATION

For the people of Israel, the Temple in Jerusalem was the place of the presence of God. All their religious festivals took place there. Jesus prayed and taught in the Temple. It was for him a house of prayer, the house of his Father, the place of meeting with God.

Now, the church is for Christians the place of meeting with God. At each celebration of the Eucharist, which takes place in the sanctuary, we participate in the heavenly liturgy. Together with the saints and the angels, we celebrate the works of God: the Father who created us, the Son who redeemed us, the Holy Spirit who gives us life.

It is God himself who invites and gathers us together, and unites us to form the Church.

THEY SERVE IN HIS SANCTUARY

The word of God in my life

When do we celebrate a feast for God?

....

What is the name of the place where we celebrate the Mass?

....

What is the sanctuary?

....

During the Mass, what do we participate in?

....

....

The Mass is a great work of love, a treasure, the most beautiful gift of Jesus to us. Why?

Underline the right answer.

because...

✳ the choir sings beautifully and I get to do a reading

✳ the Mass renews the self-offering of Jesus, full of infinite love for the Father.

✳ the church is the most important building in town.

Write the name of these objects under each photo and explain their purpose:

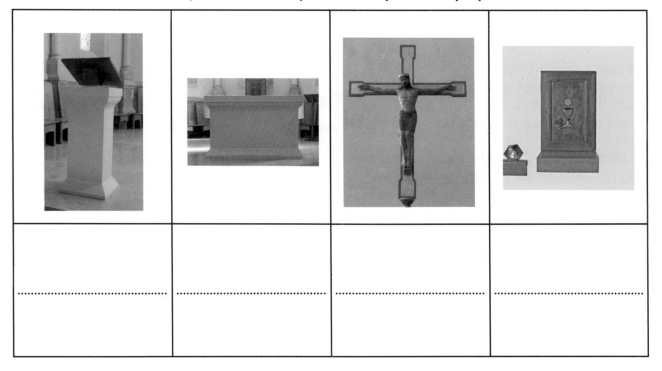

....	....	....	....

I COMMIT MYSELF to going into my parish church simply to visit Jesus present in the tabernacle.

I REMEMBER

Amen! Praise, glory, wisdom and
thanksgiving, honour, power and
strength to our God,
for ever and ever! Amen!

I pray

with the psalms

My God, I search for you.
My soul is thirsting for you, I yearn for you.
Guide my steps to your dwelling-place.
I want to draw near to your altar,
and praise you in your sanctuary.
I want to bless you with the sound of music,
sing for you with the whole assembly.

I have gazed on you in the sanctuary,
I have seen your strength and your glory.
Your love is better than life:
your praise will always be on my lips.

Happy are those who live in your house.
Happy are those who stand in your presence.
You are my king, my God,
my strength and my joy!

I sing

Hosanna, hosanna,
hosanna in the highest x2

7. THE MASS: LITURGY OF THE WORD

The Mass: *Introductory rites and Liturgy of the Word*

Each Sunday, Jesus gathers us together in church for Mass. The first part of the Mass is called the Liturgy of the Word. God speaks to us; we listen to him and we respond to him. A dialogue takes place between God and the congregation. The parable of the sower taught us to be attentive, so that the word may bear fruit. The prayers at the beginning of Mass prepare our hearts to listen.

ENTRANCE PROCESSION

Opening of the celebration and preparation

✳We stand to welcome Jesus in the person of the priest who presides at the Eucharist. The opening hymn unites our hearts in prayer. Gathered together by Jesus, we form one family.

SIGN OF THE CROSS

✳ We make the Sign of the Cross. It is by the cross that Jesus saves us. This sign is at the heart of our Christian life. We were marked with this sign on the day of our baptism and we belong to God: Father, Son and Holy Spirit. In the liturgy, we share in the life of the three persons of the Blessed Trinity.The priest asks that the grace of God be always with us. We respond: "And with your spirit".

ASKING FORGIVENESS

✳ We take a moment of silence before asking forgiveness for our sins. With the whole congregation, we pray: "I confess to Almighty God" and "Lord, have mercy". We open our hearts to receive the mercy of God.

PRAISE

✳ We sing: "Glory to God in the Highest" which unites us with the song of praise in heaven. This hymn gives joy to our hearts: "You alone are the Holy One, you alone are the Lord, we praise you, we bless you..."

PRAYER

✳ After a moment of silence, the priest gathers everyone with the opening prayer. This prayer, linked to the readings, helps us to understand the theme of the liturgy for that day.

Liturgy of the Word

The Liturgy of the Word takes place at the ambo (lectern). We all sit. Throughout the liturgical year, Sunday after Sunday, the readings help us to discover the history of salvation contained in the Bible.

FIRST READING

✳ The first reading is often taken from the Old Testament. It speaks of the love of God for his creation, for our elder brothers in the faith: Abraham, Moses, Elijah, Isaiah, Jeremiah, John the Baptist... It is the story of their call, their vocation, their faithfulness and their weaknesses. Through them, we discover the patient love of God for his people. We learn how God fulfils his promises.

PSALM

✳ The psalm also belongs to the Old Testament. It is a response to the word that God has just spoken to us in the first reading. By singing the psalm, we express to God our trust in him, our sorrow for sins, our thanksgiving and our praise. Jesus also learnt to sing the psalms in the synagogue, with his fellow countrymen and disciples.

SECOND READING

✳ The second reading belongs to the New Testament. It is often an extract from letters written by the apostles to the first Christian communities. After having preached the Gospel in one town, the apostles did not abandon the new believers. They wrote to them to encourage them in faith, supporting them in difficulties and helping them to remain faithful to the Gospel of Jesus. These letters also give us very useful advice and encouragement for living our own Christian life.

✳ We stand up to sing "Alleluia", our acclamation of joy and praise just before the Gospel. During the season of Lent, "Alleluia" is never sung or said. Then on the day of the Resurrection, Easter, and throughout Eastertide, "Alleluia" resounds again with renewed fervour.

> They went as far as Capernaum and as soon as the Sabbath came, Jesus went to the synagogue and began to teach. And his teaching made a deep impression on them because, unlike the scribes, he taught them with authority. (Mark 1: 21-22)

ALLELUIA

GOSPEL

✳The Gospel is proclaimed by the priest or deacon. The Gospels are at the heart of the scriptures. Jesus himself is this Word given to us by God. The apostles were witnesses of everything Jesus did and taught. What they heard, what they saw with their own eyes, what they touched with their hands, they have made known to us (see 1 John 1). Then this "Good News" was written down by the evangelists: Matthew, Mark, Luke and John. These books, the Gospels, are the heart of Scripture.

The Gospel, the word of God, is one way that Jesus is present with us at Mass. Like the disciples, we recognise with faith the signs and miracles that Jesus did and we believe in him, our Saviour.

"GOOD NEWS"

HOMILY

✳ The priest's homily follows on from, and is part of, the proclamation of the word of God. He explains the readings in simple words to help us understand their meaning. He calls us to live by the word so that the Holy Spirit who inspired it may transform us.

✳ The Creed is proclaimed every Sunday, the day of the Resurrection. We reaffirm the faith of our baptism, the faith of the whole Church: "I believe in God". This is our response to the word of God.

✳ The Prayer of the Faithful: we entrust to God all the intentions of the Church and the world. We pray for all those who have not been able to take part in the Eucharistic celebration. We place into the hands of our heavenly Father all those who are suffering and who rely on our prayer.

Throughout this liturgy, Jesus has "sown" his word in us. This word is all-powerful and it will bear fruit because it is the word of God. Let us keep it and cherish it in our hearts so that we may live by it and pass it on to others.

I put in order, from 1 to 13, the different moments of the Liturgy of the Word according to their order in the Mass.

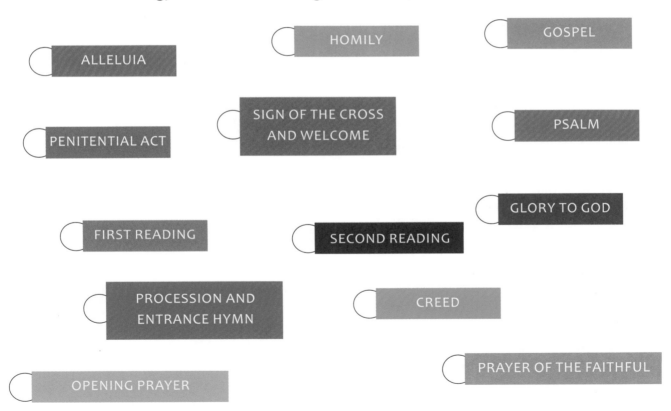

The word of God in my life

I write down a prayer intention which could be read at Mass

....

....

I COMMIT MYSELF (choose your commitment by underlining it)

- to listening attentively to the word of God at each Sunday Mass.
- to read again the word of God discovered in catechesis.

I REMEMBER

I believe in God

I believe in God, the Father almighty, Creator of heaven and earth;
and in Jesus Christ, his only Son, our Lord,
who was conceived by the Holy Spirit, born of the Virgin Mary,
suffered under Pontius Pilate, was crucified,
died and was buried; he descended into hell; on the third day he
rose again from the dead; he ascended into heaven, and is seated
at the right hand of God the Father almighty; from there he will
come to judge the living and the dead.
I believe in the Holy Spirit, the holy catholic Church, the
communion of saints, the forgiveness of sins, the resurrection of
the body and life everlasting. Amen.

I pray

Jesus, you have gathered us
to listen to your word.
We have come to you
to answer your call.
We want to listen attentively,
and let your word penetrate our hearts.

Speak Lord, I am listening!
I want to follow your counsel
to live with your life.
Give me your wisdom to know what I must do.
Pour out your love in to my heart
so that I may share it with those around me.

from Psalm 98

Sing to the Lord a new song,
for he has done wonders;
he has remembered his truth
and love,
for the house of Israel;

All the earth has seen the victory of our God.
Shout to the Lord, all the earth,
ring out, sing and play;
play for the Lord on the harp,
and on all the instruments;
with the sound of trumpet and the horn.
acclaim the King, the Lord!

I sing

Thy word is a lamp unto my feet

8. THE MASS: LITURGY OF THE EUCHARIST

The Mass: Liturgy of the Eucharist and sending out

EUCHARISTIC PRAYER

At the time he was betrayed
and entered willingly into his Passion,
he took bread and,
giving thanks,
broke it,
and gave it to his disciples, saying:

**"Take this, all of you, and eat of it,
for this is my Body, which will be given up for you."**

In a similar way, when supper was ended,
he took the chalice
and, once more giving thanks,
he gave it to his disciples, saying:

**"Take this, all of you, and drink from it,
for this is the chalice of my Blood,
the Blood of the new and eternal covenant,
which will be poured out for you and for many
for the forgiveness of sins.
Do this in memory of me."**

(From Eucharistic Prayer II)

Liturgy of the Eucharist

Each Mass is an Easter celebration, where we re-live the paschal mystery of Jesus.

- ✳ his Last Supper on Maundy Thursday
- ✳ his death on the cross
- ✳ his Resurrection.

PRESENTATION OF THE GIFTS

The liturgy of the Eucharist begins with the offertory. The priest comes to the altar. He receives the offerings brought by the faithful: bread and wine, chosen by Jesus to become his Body and Blood. These offerings are both gifts of creation and the work of human hands. The priest presents them to God*. We offer ourselves: our life, our work, the sufferings and joys of the whole of humanity.

The priest calls the assembly to pray so as to enter into the sacrifice of Jesus which gives glory to God.**

Presentation of the gifts

* Blessed are you, Lord God of all creation, for through your goodness we have received the bread we offer you: fruit of the earth and work of human hands, it will become for us the Bread of Life.

Blessed be God for ever.

Blessed are you, Lord God of all creation, for through your goodness we have received the wine...

Blessed be God for ever.

* * Pray brethren that my sacrifice and yours may be acceptable to God, the almighty Father.

May the Lord accept the sacrifice at your hands for the praise and glory of his name, for our good and the good of all his holy Church.

EUCHARISTIC PRAYER

* The Lord be with you.
And with your spirit.
Lift up your hearts.
We lift them up to the Lord.
Let us give thanks to the Lord our God.
It is right and just.

Preface
** It is truly right and just, our duty and salvation, always and everywhere to give you thanks, Father most holy, through your beloved Son, Jesus Christ...

Sanctus
*** Holy, Holy, Holy Lord God of hosts... Hosanna in the highest.

Call to the Holy Spirit
**** Make holy, therefore, these gifts, we pray, by sending down your Spirit upon them like the dewfall, so that they may become for us the Body and Blood of our Lord Jesus Christ.

PREFACE

The Eucharistic prayer is a great prayer of thanksgiving. It begins with the "Preface", a dialogue between the priest and the congregation which invites us to take part in everything that is happening on the altar*. We are happy to give thanks to the Father for all the wonders of creation and, most of all, for the amazing work accomplished through the death and resurrection of his Son, Jesus.

The priest raises his hands and sings**.

He proclaims the reasons for our praise.

At the end of the Preface, together with the angels and saints, the whole assembly acclaims the holiness of God***. Jesus is coming to be truly present on the altar.

The priest extends his hands over the bread and the chalice. He calls on the power of the Holy Spirit****. At the same time, he traces the sign of the cross over the offerings. It is by the power of the Holy Spirit and by speaking the effective words of Jesus, that the bread and the wine are going to become the Body and Blood of Christ. Jesus had asked his apostles to: "Do this in memory of me."

WORDS OF CONSECRATION

Taking the host in his hands, the priest bows and speaks the words of Jesus at the last Supper*. Then he raises high the consecrated host. I look at it: I believe Jesus is present here.

Then the priest takes the chalice, bows, and speaks the words of Jesus**. He raises up the chalice containing the consecrated wine. I look at it: I believe Jesus is present here.

With our eyes we see bread and wine. But our faith tells us: this bread is the Body of Jesus, this wine is the Blood of Jesus.

Yes, the mystery of faith is truly great***: At Mass we are near to the Cross of Jesus and at the same time we are celebrating his Resurrection.

After the consecration, the priest offers the Body and Blood of Jesus to the Father. He asks the Holy Spirit to unite all those who will be nourished by the Body of Christ at the same table****. He prays for the unity of the Church, for the pope, the bishops, the priests, for ourselves and for all people throughout the world. He also prays for the faithful departed who have left this world. The priest asks that the sacrifice of Jesus may bear fruits of salvation and peace for the whole world and obtain for us eternal life.

At the end of the Eucharistic prayer, the priest raises up the Body and Blood of Christ as he sings an acclamation*****. With the whole assembly we proclaim our faith in the mystery that has just been accomplished and we give glory to God our Father with a solemn **AMEN**.

*
"This is my body given you."

**
"This is my blood poured out for you"

***We proclaim your Death, O Lord, and profess your Resurrection until you come again.

****Humbly we pray that, partaking of the Body and Blood of Christ, we may be gathered into one by the Holy Spirit.

***** Through him, and with him, and in him, O God, almighty Father, in the unity of the Holy Spirit, all glory and honour is yours, for ever and ever.

AMEN

* Our Father who art in heaven...

Give us this day our daily bread ... deliver us from evil.

For the kingdom, the power and the glory are yours now and for ever.

** The peace

The peace of the Lord be with you always.
And with your spirit.

***Lamb of God

Lamb of God, you take away the sins of the world, have mercy on us...Grant us peace

***Communion

Behold the Lamb of God, behold him who takes away the sins of the world.
Blessed are those called to the supper of the Lamb.
Lord, I am not worthy that you should enter under my roof, but only say the word and my soul shall be healed.

COMMUNION

We prepare ourselves to receive communion by praying the Our Father*. The daily bread we are asking for is the Eucharistic bread, the Body of Christ. We ask the Father to feed us with this Bread of Life, and to purify our hearts from all wrongdoing so that we may live in unity.

The priest continues by praying for unity and peace. Then we receive from the priest the "peace of Christ"** and we pass it on to those standing near us.

The action of the "breaking of the bread" means that all those who receive Communion from this one broken bread form one body with Christ. Then the priest places a small piece of the host in the chalice as a sign of our communion with Jesus.

We ask Jesus, the Lamb of God, to have mercy on us***and then to grant us peace.

The priest invites us to come to the table of the Lord. He presents the Body of Christ to us. ****. We answer that we are not worthy to receive him.

The priest then receives the Body and the Blood of Christ in Communion. The assembly forms a procession and moves forward respectfully to receive Jesus who gives himself. As he presents the host to you, the priest will say: "The Body of Christ." You answer: "Amen", which means: "Yes, I believe that Jesus is here in Communion. He is my Lord and my God."

After communion, I can join with the assembly in singing to show my communion with the Body of Christ. Then I can pray in silence, attentive to Jesus who is dwelling in me. I remain with him.

✳ I worship Jesus. I believe in his presence,

✳ I give him thanks for so much love, and I let myself be loved by him,

✳ I entrust to him all my prayer intentions and those of the world...

✳ I offer myself to him and I commit myself to him...

Through Holy Communion, Jesus unites us to himself and to all our brothers and sisters. We form the Body of Christ.

Final blessing

With the final blessing*, we are sent out to live what we have just celebrated**. This is what the priest's prayer for us means. Renewed by the love of Christ, filled with his joy, we go out as witnesses of Jesus among our brothers and sisters, giving thanks to God.

The Eucharist transforms each moment of my life, which becomes offering, praise, sacrifice and communion.

Thanksgiving

I worship
I give thanks
I offer
I commit myself

*Blessing

May almighty God bless you, the Father, and the Son, and the Holy

Amen.

**Dismissal

Go and announce the Gospel of the Lord.

I make my own prayer to tell Jesus how much I want to receive him:

....

....

I put in order, from 1 to 7, the different moments of the Liturgy of the Eucharist according to their order in the Mass.

....

....

OUR FATHER

OFFERTORY

COMMUNION

HOLY, HOLY, HOLY

LAMB OF GOD

BLESSING AND DISMISSAL

PREFACE

I COMMIT MYSELF to making an action of communion and sharing with others.

I REMEMBER

God our Father
You feed us by giving us the bread from heaven;
Jesus, your beloved Son.
Unite us to him and transform us
through the Holy Spirit, so that we
may sing forever the wonders of your love.

I pray

Father most holy,
it is truly good to give you thanks
for the presence of Jesus among us.
Through him, with him and in him,
we praise you, we bless you, we adore you.

Jesus, take us with you
in your offering to the Father.
Your love for him is so great!
Give me the peace that only you can give.

Jesus, you want to make your home in my heart.
I am not worthy that you should come to me,
but I am longing to receive you.

Jesus, I want you to be my food and my friend.
I want to live as a witness of your love
to everyone I meet.

I want to continue to live from the Eucharist
through praise, prayer,
and the offering of my whole life.

I sing

Be still for the presence of the Lord

I MUST STAY AT YOUR HOUSE TODAY

9. WELCOMING JESUS LIKE ZACCHAEUS

Jesus comes to me

THE WORD OF GOD

LUKE 19:1-10

01 [Jesus] entered Jericho and was going through the town when 02 a man whose name was Zacchaeus made his appearance. He was one of the senior tax collectors and a wealthy man. 03 He was anxious to see what kind of man Jesus was, but he was too short and could not see him for the crowd; 04 so he ran ahead and climbed a sycamore tree to catch a glimpse of Jesus, who was to pass that way. 05 When Jesus reached the spot, he looked up and spoke to him:

"Zacchaeus, come down. Hurry, because I must stay at your house today." 06 And he hurried down and welcomed him joyfully.

07 They all complained when they saw what was happening. "He has gone to stay at a sinner's house," they said. 08 But Zacchaeus stood his ground and said to the Lord, "Look, sir, I am going to give half my property to the poor, and if I have cheated anybody, I will pay him back four times the amount."

09 And Jesus said to him, "Today salvation has come to this house, because this man too is a son of Abraham; 10 for the Son of Man has come to seek out and save what was lost."

I welcome the word of God

Zacchaeus desires to see Jesus. He wants to know him because he has heard about him. The crowd prevents Zacchaeus from reaching Jesus, but he does not get discouraged. He climbs on a tree to see Jesus. Jesus stops. He raises his eyes and looks at Zacchaeus and calls him by name: "Zacchaeus, I must stay at your house today."

ZACCHAEUS RECEIVES JESUS WITH JOY

The look of Jesus is God's look of love on Zacchaeus. Jesus knows that in the midst of the crowd there is one person, Zacchaeus, who is in special need of him.

"And he hurried down." Zacchaeus obeys at once. What joy for him to welcome Jesus into his house! The people do not understand Jesus' decision: "He has gone to stay at a sinner's house" The people

HALF OF WHAT I OWN, LORD, I WILL GIVE TO THE POOR

despise Zacchaeus because of his wrongdoings. He is even rejected by those who think they are righteous. But Jesus' mission is to save everyone. He is not afraid to go and meet sinners.

Zacchaeus discovers Jesus' love for him. In Jesus' presence, Zacchaeus becomes aware of what is stopping him from being happy, and living in peace with God and with others. He makes an important decision: he will make up for the wrong he has done and share his possessions with the poor. This is a true conversion! It does not come from him but from the Lord who lifts him up.

"Salvation has come to this house today."

Jesus lets everyone know what he has done in the heart of Zacchaeus. Jesus has restored Zacchaeus in God's covenant of love with his people. By welcoming Jesus, Zacchaeus has welcomed salvation, the life of God.

The word of God in my life

What did Zacchaeus want most of all?

....

What about you? Is there something you would like to tell Jesus about?

....

....

Choose and write down in the windows of the house what you want Jesus to pour out in the "house" of your heart.

GOODNESS – **LOVE** – **PATIENCE** – **TRUTH** – **CHARITY** – **FAITH** –

TRUST – **OBEDIENCE** – **COURAGE**

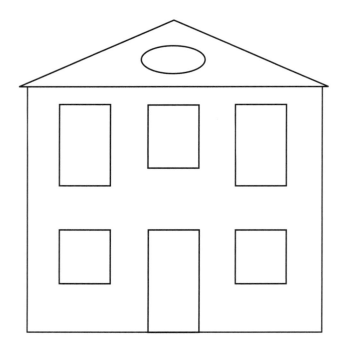

I COMMIT MYSELF to take Jesus' coming seriously.
I will tell him often:
"Come, Jesus, I am waiting for you."

Salvation has come to this house today.

Colour the words of Jesus to Zacchaeus

I REMEMBER

Look, I am standing at the door, and knocking. If you hear my call, and open the door, I will come in to you, and have supper with you, and you, with me.

(Revelation 3:20)

I sing

There was a man in Jericho called Zacchaeus

I pray

Jesus, you look at me with love.
You want to stay with me.
You do not worry about my weakness and my sin.
You have come to seek and save what was lost.
Jesus, you know that I need you.

You want to make your home in me
and transform my whole life.
I want to prepare the house of my heart.
Yes, Jesus, come!
Fill me with your love.
Strengthen me to do your will,
so that my heart may be fully yours.

O Jesus,
soon I will have the joy
of receiving you in the Eucharist!
You will make me one with you.
You will make my heart big enough
to hold your great love
for the Church and the world.

In the joy of receiving you,
I will tell everyone:
"Today, Jesus has come into my heart!"

STAY WITH US

10. JESUS WALKS WITH US

The pilgrims of Emmaus

THE WORD OF GOD

LUKE 24:13-35

[13] That very same day, two [followers of Jesus] were on their way to a village called Emmaus, seven miles from Jerusalem, [14] and they were talking together about all that had happened.

[15] Now as they talked this over, Jesus himself approached came up and walked by their side; [16] but something prevented them from recognising him. [17] He said to them, "What matters are you discussing as you walk along?" They stopped short, their faces downcast. [18] Then one of them, called Cleopas, answered him, "You must be the only person staying in Jerusalem who does not know the things that have been happening there these last few days." [19] "What things?" he asked. "All about Jesus of Nazareth" they answered "Who proved he was a great prophet by the things he said and did in the sight of God and of the whole people; [20] and how our chief priests and our leaders handed him over to be sentenced to death, and had him crucified. [21] Our own hope had been that he would be the one to set Israel free. And this is not all: two whole days have gone by since it all happened; [22] and some women from our group have astounded us: they went to the tomb in the early morning, [23] and when they did not find the body, they came back to tell us they had seen a vision of angels, who declared he was alive. [24] Some of our friends went to the tomb and found everything exactly as the women had reported, but of him they saw nothing."

[25] Then he said to them, "You foolish men! So slow to believe the full message of the prophets! [26] Was it not ordained that the Christ should suffer and so enter into his glory?" [27] Then, starting with Moses, and going through all the prophets, he explained to them the passages throughout the scriptures that were about himself. [28] When they drew near to the village to which they were going, he made as if to go on; [29] but they pressed him to stay with them, "It is nearly evening" they said "and the day is almost over." So he went in to stay with them. [30] Now while he was with them at table, he took the bread and said the blessing; then he broke it and handed it to them. [31] And their eyes were opened, and they recognised him; but he had vanished from their sight. [32] Then they said to each other, "Did not our hearts burn within us as he talked to us on the road and explained the scriptures to us?" [33] They set out that instant and returned to Jerusalem. There, they found the Eleven assembled together with their companions, [34] who said to them, "Yes, it is true. the Lord has risen and has appeared to Simon." [35] Then they told their story of what had happened on the road and how they had recognised him, at the breaking of bread.

I welcome the word of God

Two disciples, overcome with grief by the death of Jesus, are walking towards Emmaus. They had been filled with wonder at his words and actions and had placed all their trust in him. Now their faith has crumbled after these events. Jesus comes and joins them, takes an interest in them and starts a conversation. First he listens to them

THEY PRESSED HIM TO STAY WITH THEM

and then explains what the prophets had foretold about the Saviour Messiah: why Christ suffered and died. Jesus is patient with the two disciples because he wants them to grow in faith. He does not show himself in his risen glory. Jesus prepares their hearts and waits for the best moment to reveal to them that he himself is the Christ.

The disciples are comforted by the presence and the words of this strange companion. Their hearts gradually open up to a glimmer of hope. They would love to have more time with him! "They pressed him to stay with them!" Jesus accepts their invitation and goes in to stay with them.

It is at the breaking of the bread that they recognise Jesus, the Lord! He is alive, he has truly risen!

Once Jesus has vanished, the disciples are struck with wonder and reminisce about the experience they have just had. The words of Jesus touched their hearts. Jesus has rekindled in them the fire of their love. Their faith in the risen Jesus lifts their spirits again and puts them back on their feet. It is late, but they cannot keep such joyful news to themselves! They set off to join the other disciples in Jerusalem, their hearts burning with love.

Just like the apostles, the disciples of Emmaus become witnesses of the Resurrection. Now, they can affirm that they have seen Jesus alive, that he walked with them and that they recognised him in the breaking of the bread.

Which village is the disciples walking towards?

....

What is the name of one of the disciples?

....

....

Gather together the words that tell us how the disciples felt:

joyful – discouraged – sad – despairing – astonished – filled with hope – burning hearts
– slow to believe – witnesses – questioning – slow to understand – believers.

Before meeting Jesus	**After** meeting Jesus

When do the disciples feel their hearts burning within them?

....

When do the disciples recognise the risen Jesus?

....

Why do they return to Jerusalem?

....

The word of God in my life

We experience the meeting of the two disciples with Jesus at each Mass.

Match the main moments of Mass with their corresponding sentences from the Gospel:

The disciples of Emmaus	The Mass
1. Jesus himself came up and walked by their side.	1.
2. He explained to them everything in the scriptures concerning himself.	2.
3. When they were at table, he took the bread, said the blessing, broke it, and handed it to them.	3.
4. They immediately set out and returned to Jerusalem... then told what had happened on the road	4.

I COMMIT MYSELF AND I REMEMBER:

I want to listen to the words of Jesus and receive his body,
the Bread of Life.
Then my heart can burn with love
like the disciples of Emmaus.
Strengthened in my baptismal life,
I will become a witness of the risen Jesus.

I pray

Jesus, you are present in each one of us.
You live in our hearts
from the moment of our baptism.
You are our companion on the journey.

You are present in your word.
We want to welcome your word
and be taught by you.
May your word make our hearts burn within us.

Jesus, you are truly present here
in the Eucharist.
I do not see you, you are hidden.
I do not hear you, you are silent.
You are here for us, in the tabernacle.
This I believe.

Stay with us, Jesus.
Listen to our prayer.
Do not leave us.

We worship you, and we say THANK YOU!
We want to love you as you have loved us.
Give us hearts burning with love
to tell to everyone that you are risen!

I sing

This is the Body, This is the Blood

I AM THE VINE, YOU ARE THE BRANCHES

11. UNITED WITH JESUS FOR THE CHURCH

The Eucharist unites us with Jesus

THE WORD OF GOD

JOHN 15:1-8

[01] I am the true vine, and my Father is the vinedresser. [02] Every branch in me that bears no fruit he cuts away, and every branch that does bear fruit he prunes to make it bear even more.

[04] Make your home in me, as I make mine in you...

[05] I am the vine, you are the branches. Whoever remains in me, with me in him, bears fruit in plenty; for cut off from me you can do nothing. [06] Anyone who does not remain in me is like a branch that has been thrown away – he withers...
[08] It is to the glory of my Father that you should bear much fruit, and then you will be my disciples.

I welcome the word of God

Jesus often used parables to explain the mysteries of the kingdom of heaven. He also used images to talk about himself and to help us to know him better:

✳ **I am** ....

✳ **I am** ....

✳ **I am** ....

✳ **I am** ....

On the evening of Maundy Thursday, during the Last Supper with his disciples, Jesus reveals to them how much he loves them and the deep bonds which unite them to him by using the image of the vine.

In this Gospel, Jesus also speaks about his Father.

To whom does Jesus compare the Father?

....

To what does he compare his disciples?

....

"Make your home in me as I make mine in you"

Explain these words of Jesus

....

....

The word of God in my life

How can I remain united to Jesus?

....

....

Write down the name of a saint, of someone who was a friend of God

✳ who gave his or her life for people who were poor :...

✳ who travelled far away to evangelise: ....

✳ who withdrew from the world in order to live with God alone: ....

✳ who simply lived a good Christian life in his or her family : ....

I COMMIT MYSELF to following Jesus, like the saints, by

....

I REMEMBER

Whoever remains in me with me in him, bears fruit in plenty;
for cut off from me you can do nothing.

I pray

Jesus, you are the true vine,
we are the branches.
You are our life.
Jesus, come and live in me,
so that I may love with your love,
so that I may look at others with your eyes.
Without you, Jesus, without your Spirit of love,
   I can do nothing.

Jesus, I desire to receive you in the Eucharist.
Come and live in me, so that I may live in you.
May I be more and more united to you!
I want to remain in your love.
May I never be separated from you!

Jesus, I want to work for your Church.
I want to bear the fruit that the Father expects
   of me: goodness, patience, joy...

Jesus, help us all to become saints
for the glory of the Father
and the joy of the Holy Spirit.

Mary, Jesus lived in you.
Teach us to live in Jesus.
Mary, queen of all the saints, pray for us.

I sing

This is my Body, broken for you

12. MARY, MOTHER OF THE BREAD OF LIFE

Celebration

Mary, beloved of the Most High,
God has chosen you from all eternity to be the mother of his Son.
God has filled you with his love and his life, with his joy and his light!
You said "yes" when the angel Gabriel, asked you on behalf of the Lord
to be the mother of the Son of God.

Through the power of the Spirit who covered you with his shadow, and through your loving "yes"
to this unexpected message,
the Word of God was made flesh in you,
Emmanuel, God with us, found a place in you
and made his home in you.

Through your faith, you became the ark of the covenant, the tabernacle of the Most High.
You carried in secret the salvation of the world.
So your soul was filled with joyful praise at the wonders
that the Lord almighty has accomplished in you: "Great is the Lord!"

You became the soil
where the small seed of the Word of God grew.
Through you, God became a little child and you gave Jesus to the world:
Jesus, the Lamb of God, the Saviour!
From the manger to the Cross and to the Resurrection, you walked with Jesus.
His words were the food to satisfy your hunger,
and you pondered them in your heart.

Through your faith, your love and your hope, you have shared in the work of salvation.
You, his mother, became his disciple.
Mary, mother of Christ and of the Church, give us Jesus, the Bread of Life!

I sing

As I kneel before you

13. THE DAY OF MY FIRST HOLY COMMUNION

Jesus, you make your home in me

Jesus, how I have longed for you to come to me!
You are here, living in me.
You have made your home in me.

You are the Son of God and the son of Mary,
you whom the apostles have seen and touched,
you whom the angels worship in heaven, you are here! I believe it.
Jesus, you are the Bread of Life.

I want to stay close to you and adore you, I want to be attentive to your presence!
Look at me, Jesus.
Give me your life and your love!
Keep me always close to you!
May I love you with all my heart.

How can I thank you, Jesus?
I want to work for you,
to make you known and loved.

Filled with joy today, I want to tell everyone: Jesus is alive in me!
I have received him for the first time!
Rejoice with me because Jesus loves me and will always love me!

Today,   /   /

(write the date)

in my parish church of

_____

(write the name of your parish)

I received Jesus for the first time in the
sacrament of the Eucharist

_____

(you can sign your name)

Thank you Jesus for my first Holy Communion!
Give me the joy of receiving you often!

I Want to
Make my
Home in You

redemptorist
publications

ISBN-13: 978-0-85231-490-6

9 780852 314906